# America The Bold, America The Brave, America The Beautiful

*Vol II*

Ronda Sexton

Copyright © 2022 Ronda Sexton

All rights reserved

No part of this book may be reproduced, or stored in a retrieval system, or transmitted in any form or by any means, electronic, mechanical, photocopying, recording, or otherwise, without express written permission of the publisher.

ISBN-979-8-9927639-3-5
Registration Number:TXu 2-324-850

Cover design by: GenArt {AI Software}
Library of Congress Control Number: 2018675309
Printed in the United States of America

# Contents

Title Page
Copyright
Hawaii     1
Idaho     26
Illinois     52
Indiana     77
Iowa     103
Kansas     129
Kentucky     155
Louisiana     182
Maine     209
Maryland     235

*Love the world as your own self; then you can truly care for all things* – Lao Tzu

## The Connecticut State Library Gave Me Some Really Good Information, I Felt I Should Share With You.

In 45 B.C., Julius Caesar ordered a calendar consisting of twelve months based on a solar year. This calendar employed a cycle of three years of 365 days, followed by a year of 366 days (leap year). When first implemented, the "Julian Calendar" also moved the beginning of the year from March 1 to January 1. However, following the fall of the Roman Empire in the fifth century, the new year was gradually realigned to coincide with Christian festivals until by the seventh century, Christmas Day marked the beginning of the new year in many countries.

In accordance with a 1750 act of Parliament, England and its colonies changed calendars in 1752. By that time, the discrepancy between a solar year and the Julian Calendar had grown by an additional day, so that the calendar used in England and its colonies was 11 days out-of-sync with the Gregorian Calendar in use in most other parts of Europe.

England's calendar change included three major components. The Julian Calendar was replaced by the Gregorian Calendar, changing the formula for calculating leap years. The beginning of the legal new year was moved from March 25 to January 1. Finally, 11 days were dropped from the month of September 1752.

The changeover involved a series of steps:

December 31, 1750 was followed by January 1, 1750 (under the "Old Style" calendar, December was the 10th month and January the 11th)

March 24, 1750 was followed by March 25, 1751 (March 25 was the first day of the "Old Style" year)

December 31, 1751 was followed by January 1, 1752 (the switch from March 25 to January 1 as the first day of the year)

September 2, 1752 was followed by September 14, 1752 (drop of 11 days to conform to the Gregorian calendar)

**Ct State Library: Colonial Records & Topics; Received Dec 30,2022**


Also, all land measurements are estimated. The actual dimensions of all natural landmarks are based on the area in which they are measured and the equipment used to do so. Information, I have given are based on a variety of books {some written in the past, other more recent} and within a 5% margin of error compared to other sources.

# Hawaii

RONDA SEXTON

*"Hawaii: a living masterpiece, where emerald mountains rise from turquoise seas, and each sunset paints the sky with colors that capture the soul, reminding us of nature's boundless splendor."*

CHATGPT {AI Generator}

AMERICA THE BOLD, AMERICA THE BRAVE, AMERICA THE BEAUTIFUL

## *Hawaii Stats*

## Statehood:

Date Granted: August 21, 1959
Rank of Admission: Hawaii became the 50th state to join the United States

## State Capital:

Capital City: Honolulu {Honolulu County}
Adopted date: August 31, 1850 {Territorial capital}
Adopted date: August 21, 1959 {Date of Admission}
Capitol Building Design Architect(s):
Belt, Lemmon & Lo {Current Building}
John Carl Warnecke & Associates {Current Building}

## State Population:

Population: 1,455,271 {US Federal Census 2020}
Rank: 40th most populous in the United States

## Land Mass:

Total Land Mass: 6,459 square miles {16,728.733 square kilometers}
Rank: 47th in Rank of The Largest State(s) in the United States

***Hawaii is continually growing; therefore, total square miles will become inaccurate over time*****

AMERICA THE BOLD, AMERICA THE BRAVE, AMERICA THE BEAUTIFUL

## Lovely Weather of Hawaii

### Record Highest Temperature:

Date: April 27, 1931
Location: Pahala {Hawaii Island}
Temperature: 100 degrees Fahrenheit {37.78 degrees Celsius}

### Record Lowest Temperature:

Date: May 17, 1979
Location: Mauna Kea Observatory {Hawaii Island}
Temperature: 12 degrees Fahrenheit {-11.11 degrees Celsius}

### Record Snowfall:

Date: February 2, 1936
Location: Haleakala {Maui Island}
Amount: 6.5 inches {16.51 centimeters} (within a 24-hour time frame)

## Record Precipitation:

Date: April 14–15, 2018
Location: Waipa Garden {Kauai Island}
Amount: 49.69 inches {126.21 centimeters} (within a 24-hour time frame)

## Major Earthquake:

Date: April 2, 1868
Location: Kaʻū {Hawaii Island}
Magnitude: 7.9 {Richter Scale}

RONDA SEXTON

*Hawaii Pride*

### State Name Origin:

Hawaii derived from the Native Hawaiian word "Owhyhee" meaning "Homeland"

### State Nickname(S):

Paradise of the Pacific
The Aloha State
The Pineapple State

### State Slogan:

The Aloha State

### State Motto:

"Ua Mau ke Ea o ka 'Äina i ka Pono" {The Life of the Land is Perpetuated in Righteousness}

RONDA SEXTON

# Symbols of Hawaii

AMERICA THE BOLD, AMERICA THE BRAVE, AMERICA THE BEAUTIFUL

**State Bird:**

Nene {Hawaiian Goose}
"Branta sandvicensis"
Adopted date: May 7, 1957

## State Flag:

Designed by: Unknown {Requested by King Kamehameha}
***Newspaper article from 1845 gave credit to a Captain Hunt of the Her British Majesty Ship.
Adopted date: December 29, 1845

**State Flower:**

Ma'ohauhele {Yellow Hibiscus}
"Hibiscus Brackenridgei"
Adopted date: June 6, 1988

**State Quarter:**

Released date: November 3, 2008
50th quarter released, honoring all 50 states
Themed: "Ua Mau Ke Ea O Ka 'Aina I Ka Pono" {The life of the land is perpetuated in righteousness}
Highlights: Kamehameha, the first king of Hawaii
Designed by: Don Everhart
Engraved by: Don Everhart

**State Song:**

Hawai'i Pono'i
Written by: King David Kalakaua
Composed by: Henry Berger
Adopted date: June 13, 1967

RONDA SEXTON

**State Tree:**

Kukui {Candlenut Tree}
"Aleurites moluccana"
Adopted date: May 1, 1959

## Hawaii Facts

## Twenty Interesting Facts About Hawaii

1. The state of Hawaii is primarily formed by eight main islands. Hawaii Island, with an estimated area of 4,028 square miles {10,432.472 square kilometers}, is the largest island. Maui Island is the 2nd largest island, with an area of approximately 727.2 square miles {1,883.439 square kilometers}. O'ahu Island is the 3rd largest island, with an estimated area of 596.7 square miles {1,545.446 square kilometers}. Kaua'i Island is the 4th largest island, with a total area of approximately 562.3 square miles {1,456.350 square kilometers}. Moloka'i is the 5th largest island, with an area of approximately 260 square miles {673.397 square kilometers}. Lāna'i Island is the 6th largest island, with an estimated area of 140.5 square miles {363.893 square kilometers}. Ni'ihau Island is the 7th largest island, with an estimated area of 69.5 square miles {180.004 square kilometers}. Kaho'olawe Island is the 8th largest island, with an area of approximately 44.59 square miles {115.488 square kilometers}.

2. Geographically, when measured from east to west, Hawaii is the second-widest state in the United States, growing by an estimated 42 acres {16.997 hectares} per year. Hawaii is the southernmost state in the United States and is the only American state not located in North America. The state is an estimated 2,390 miles {3,846.33 kilometers} from California; approximately 3,850 miles {6,195.97 kilometers} from Japan; an estimated 4,900 miles {7,885.79 kilometers} from China; and an estimated 5,280 miles {8,497.34 kilometers} from the Philippines.

3. Kaho'olawe Island, nicknamed the Target Isle, is the only island that has no permanent residents {due to the lack of fresh water}. During WWII until 1990, Kaho'olawe Island was

primarily used for training purposes by the United States Armed Forces. Currently, the island is primarily used by the Native Hawaiians for cultural and spiritual purposes.

4. The Hawaiian language features many unique qualities. The Hawaiian alphabet consists of 13 letters. Vowels include the letters {A, E, I, O, U} along with the 'okina {'}. Consonants consist of the letters H, K, L, M, N, P, and W.

5. Ala Kahakai National Historic Trail is an estimated 175-mile {281.635-kilometer} trail located on the island of Hawaii. The trail is broken up into several segments along the coastline. Ala Kahakai means "Shoreline Trail" in the Hawaiian language and follows the ancient fisherman's trails through an estimated 200 ahupua'a {a traditional sea to mountain land division}.

6. Hawaii has its own time zone, {Hawaiian Standard Time, or HST}. There is no daylight savings time. Hawaiian Standard Time is five hours behind Eastern Standard Time and two hours behind Pacific Standard Time.

7. Akaka Falls State Park, located in Honomū {Hawaii County}, features two of Hawaii's natural waterfalls. The Akaka Falls is an estimated 442-foot {134.721-meter} waterfall that cascades into a gorge below. The Kahuna Falls is an estimated 400-foot {121.92-meter} waterfall featuring numerous smaller cascades.

8. Hawaii has six active volcanoes: Lo'ihi {also known as Kama'ehuakanaloa} is located underwater approximately 22 miles {35.41 kilometers} off the southeast coast of the island of Hawaii; Also located on the Hawaii Island are Kīlauea, Mauna Loa, Mauna Kea, and Hualālai. Haleakalā is located on the Maui Island. Of the six, Kīlauea {eruptions occur approximately every 2 to 3 years} and Mauna Loa {eruptions occur approximately every 5 years} are two of the world most active volcanoes.

9. A section of Kealakekua Bay {Hawaii Island} is owned by the British government. On February 14, 1779, an English explorer was killed on the bay. The Hawaiian royal family erected a monument in his honor, dedicating it to the British government. To date, the monument and the land it sits upon belong to the British government.

10. Kaua'i Island, {nicknamed the Garden Isle}, is considered one of the wettest spots on the earth. On average, the east side of Mount Wai'ale'ale {a shield volcano}, receives an estimated 466 inches, or 1,183.64 centimeters {exact amount is unknown} of rain per year.

11. Haleakala Crater is a massive shield volcano located on the island of Maui. The tallest peak of the crater is the Pu'u'Ula'ula Peak {Red Hill}. The peak features an elevation of approximately 10,023 feet {3,055.010 meters} and a prominence of an estimated 10,023 feet {3,055.010 meters}. Haleakala Crater covers an estimated 75 percent of the island and is the world's largest dormant volcano.

12. Moloka'i Island, commonly known as "The Friendly Isle", contains the world's highest sea cliffs, Hawaii's second tallest waterfall {Pu'uka'oku Falls}, and the largest fringing reef {type of coral reef} in the United States {an estimated 25 miles or 40.234 kilometers long}.

13. Hawaii is full of magical and mysterious creatures, from the Huaka'ipo {Night Marchers} to the demigod Kamapua'a. The island of Kaua'i has the legend of the Menehune. The Menehune are dwarf-like creatures, measuring between an estimated 6 inches to 2 feet {15.24 centimeters to 0.610 meters} in height. They reside in the lush forests and enjoy dancing, singing, and archery. The Menehune are known to have magic arrows that pierce the hearts of angry people, making them feel instant loving feelings. The creatures are also known to have excellent

craftsmanship and great strength, constructing temples, fish ponds, roads, canoes, and houses. According to legend, the Alekoko Fishpond was created by the Menehune in one single night.

14. The Wailuku River is the longest and largest river in Hawaii. The river is approximately 28 miles {45.062 kilometers} in length. The lower section of the river is used for the generation of hydroelectricity due to the average flow of approximately 275 cubic feet {7.787 cubic meters} per second. Along the river are the famous Rainbow Falls {an estimated 80 feet or 24.384 meters waterfall} and the Boiling Pots {a section of the Wailuku River that become turbulent after the river rises}.

15. Standing approximately 13,796 feet {4,205.021 meters} above sea level, Mauna Kea is Hawaii's tallest mountain. However, the base of the mountain stretches an estimated 19,673 feet {5,996.330 meters} below the Pacific Ocean, making Mauna Kea the tallest mountain in the United States at an estimated 33,476 feet {10,203.485 meters}.

16. Hawaii features several waterfalls that are among the top twenty in the world. The Olo'upena Falls {Moloka'i Island}, with a height of approximately 2,953 feet {900.074 meters}, is the tallest waterfall in the United States and the fourth tallest in the world {unofficially}. Pu'uka'oku Falls {Moloka'i Island}, with a height of approximately 2,756 feet {840.029 meters}, is the 2nd tallest in the United States and the 8th tallest in the world. Waihilau Falls {Hawaii Island}, with a height of approximately 2,598 feet {791.870 meters}, is the 3rd tallest in the United States and the 13th tallest waterfall in the world.

17. The Hilina Slump is an estimated 4,760-cubic mile {19,840.55-cubic kilometer} section of the south slope of the Kīlauea Volcano {Hawaii Island}. On November 29, 1975, an estimated 40-mile {64.374-kilometer} wide section of the Hilina

Slump dropped approximately 11 feet {3.353 meters} and slid an estimated 26 feet {7.925 meters} toward the ocean. The slide caused a 7.2-magnitude earthquake and an estimated 47-foot {14.326-meter} tsunami. In Punaluʻu {Honolulu County}, oceanfront properties were knocked off their foundations. Two fatalities were reported in Halapē {Hawaii County}, and an estimated 19 others reported injuries.

18. Lānaʻi Island, referred to as the Pineapple Isle, is 98% privately owned. The island is approximately 18 miles {28.969 kilometers} wide and almost circular. Located on the island is Mount Lānaʻihale, an inactive volcano with an elevation of an estimated 3,366 feet {1,025.957 meters}.

19. On December 7, 1941, an Imperial Japanese Navy airplane and midget submarines attacked a United States Navy base, Pearl Harbor, located on the island of Oʻahu. More than 180 US aircraft were destroyed, and 2,335 military personnel {including 2,008 Navy personnel, 109 Marines, and 218 Army} were killed. On December 8, 1941 {in Tokyo}, Japan declared war on the United States and the British Empire. Due to the attack not being done without a declaration of war and a warning, the attack on Pearl Harbor was determined to be a war crime on November 12, 1948, by the Tokyo Trial {International Military Tribunal for the Far East}. In 2016, the Japanese Prime Minister visited the harbor during the 75th anniversary of the attack.

20. There are approximately 12 rivers in Hawaii. Kauaʻi Island has the most rivers of all the islands {Hanalei River, Hanapēpē River, Huleʻia River, Kalihiwai River, Lumahaʻi River, Wailua River, Waimea River}. Wailua River is the largest and only navigable river in Hawaii. Huleia is the longest river and is suitable for kayaking. Oʻahu Island has two rivers {the Anahulu River and Waimea River}. Maui Island features the Waihee River. {Maui Island}. The Wailuku River is located on the Hawaii Island, and Wailau River is located on the Molokai Island.

AMERICA THE BOLD, AMERICA THE BRAVE, AMERICA THE BEAUTIFUL

# What Was Hawaii Thinking

## Ten Crazy Laws In Hawaii

1. All public schools are required to have a Hawaiian language medium education program.

2. No court, official, public servant, or public employee may declare any farming operation a nuisance.

3. Maui County banned all marble games for minors under the age of 18.

4. Coqui frogs are designated as an invasive species and are banned from the island{s}.

5. Billboards are prohibited.

6. In 2013, Honolulu lawmakers passed a bill to ban excessive feeding of feral birds. The bill took effect on July 1, 2024.

7. Hawaii banned all "powdered" alcohol.

8. It is unlawful for any minor to be in a public place after the hours of 8 pm in Maui County.

9. A person can face up to one year in jail for possessing a shark fin.

10. All dental students must be residents of the State of Hawaii.

****Please note, these laws may no longer be on the books; however, they were a law during some point in Hawaii's history****

# Idaho

*"Idaho's beauty is a quiet symphony, where rugged mountains, crystal-clear rivers, and vast open skies remind us that nature's finest work is often found in its most untouched places."*

CHATGPT {AI Generator}

RONDA SEXTON

# Idaho Stats

## Statehood:

Date Granted: July 3, 1890
Rank of Admission: Idaho became the 43rd state to join the United States.

## State Capital:

Capital City: Boise {Ada County}
Adopted date: December 24, 1864
Capitol Building Design Architect(s):
John E. Tourtellotte {Current Building}
Charles Hummel {Current Building}

## State Population:

Population: 1,839,106 {US Federal Census 2020}
Rank: 38th most populous in the United States

## Land Mass:

Total Land Mass: 83,574 square miles {216,455.67 square kilometers}
Rank: 14th in Rank of The Largest State(s) in the United States

RONDA SEXTON

## *Lovely Weather in Idaho*

### Record Highest Temperature:

Date: July 28, 1934
Location: Orofino {Clearwater County}
Temperature: 118 degrees Fahrenheit {47.78 degrees Celsius}

### Record Lowest Temperature:

Date: January 18, 1943
Location: Island Park Dam {Fremont County}
Temperature: -60 degrees Fahrenheit {-51.11 degrees Celsius}

### Record Snowfall:

Date: May 2, 1983
Location: Silver City {Owyhee County}
Amount: 60 inches {152.4 centimeters} (within a 24-hour timeframe)

### Record Snowfall:

Date: January 22, 1982
Location: Tensed {Benewah County}
Amount: 60 inches {152.4 centimeters} (within a 24-hour timeframe)

### Record Precipitation:

Date: November 23, 1909
Location: Rattlesnake Creek {Elmore County}
Amount: 7.17 inches {18.212 centimeters} (within a 24-hour timeframe)

### Major Earthquake:

Date: October 28, 1983
Location: Custer County {Borah Peak}
Magnitude: 6.9 {Richter Scale}

AMERICA THE BOLD, AMERICA THE BRAVE, AMERICA THE BEAUTIFUL

## Idaho Pride

## State Name Origin:

Idaho derives from the Nez Perce Native Indian term meaning "The Land of Many Waters"

## State Nickname(S):

The Gem State
Gem of the Mountains
Little Ida

## State Slogan:

The Gem State

## State Motto:

"Esto perpetua" {It is Perpetual}

AMERICA THE BOLD, AMERICA THE BRAVE, AMERICA THE BEAUTIFUL

# Symbols of Idaho

RONDA SEXTON

## State Bird:

Mountain Bluebird
"Sialia Arctcia"
Adopted date: February 28, 1931

**State Flag:**

Designed by: Replica of the Idaho State Seal
Adopted date: March 12, 1907

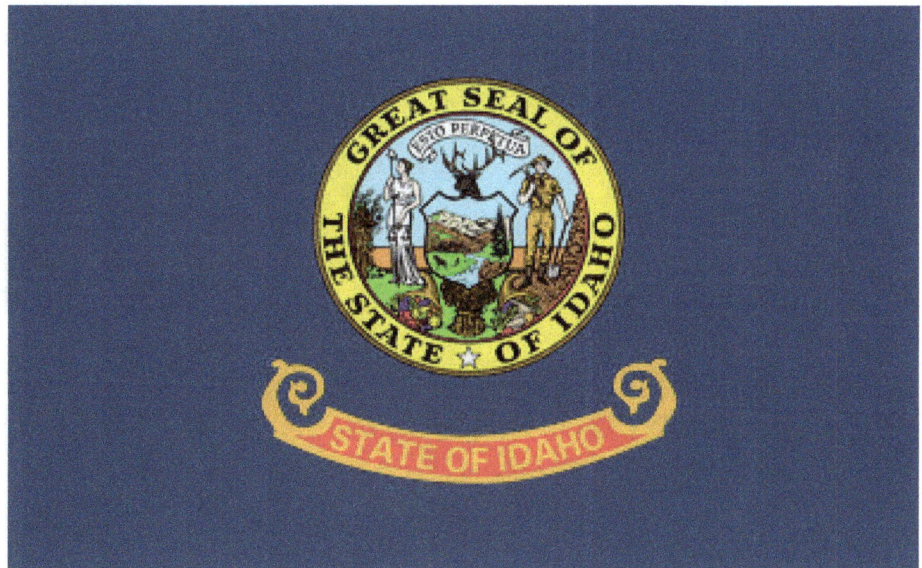

RONDA SEXTON

**State Flower:**

Syringa
"Philadelphus lewisii"
Adopted date: March 2, 1931

**State Quarter:**

Released date: June 4, 2007
43rd quarter released, honoring all 50 states
Themed: "Esto Perpetua" {Let it be perpetual}
Highlights: Peregrine Falcon, outline of the state of Idaho
Designed by: Don Everhart
Engraved by: Donna Weaver

**State Song:**

Here We Have Idaho
Written by: McKinley Helm and Albert J Tompkins
Composed by: Sallie Hume Douglas
Adopted date: March 11, 1931

## State Tree:

White Pine
"Pinus Monticolae"
Adopted date: February 13, 1935

RONDA SEXTON

## Idaho Facts

## Twenty Interesting Facts About Idaho

1. The Port of Lewiston {Nez Perce County} is approximately 465 miles {748.34 kilometers} from the Pacific Ocean. However, the ocean is accessible by traveling through the Snake River and the Columbia River. It takes an estimated 50 hours to travel from Lewiston {Nez Perce County} to Portland {Multnomah County}, Oregon by barge, or about 6 hours by automobile.

2. At approximately 7:30 a.m. on June 5, 1976, while being filled for the first time, an engineer noticed a small leak appearing on the dam walls of the Teton Dam {Fremont and Madison Counties}. By 9:30 a.m., an estimated 20 to 30 cubic feet {0.566 to 0.850 cubic meters} per second of water had begun discharging. Despite the efforts of bulldozer operators, by 11:00 a.m., the dam released approximately one million cubic feet per second of water. At 11:15 a.m., the local media informed the county sheriff's office to evacuate residents in the downstream cities. At 11:55 a.m., the crest of the dam collapsed, spilling over two million cubic feet per second of water into the Teton River canyon. The dam break destroyed thousands of homes and businesses in several cities. Many newspapers reported 11 human fatalities, while some articles noted 14 fatalities. In total, the federal government paid over $322 million {USD} in damages {some claims estimated total damages as high as 2 billion USD}, whereas the dam's construction cost was $100 million {USD}. To date, the dam has never been rebuilt.

3. Trinity Mountain has the highest fire lookout {Elmore County} in the Boise National Forest. The fire lookout stands at an estimated 9,451 feet {2,880.667 meters}.

4. The Dworshak Reservoir {Clearwater County} is approximately 50 miles {80.467 kilometers} long. Located

within the reservoir is a concrete gravity dam, commonly known as the Dworshak Dam. The Dworshak Dam stands at an estimated 717 feet {218.542 meters}, making it the third-tallest dam in the United States and the tallest straight-axis concrete dam in the Western Hemisphere to date.

5. Grangeville {Idaho County} is located on the Camas Prairie and is considered the gateway to six rivers, five wilderness areas, and four national forests. To the south of the city is the Nez Perce National Forest, established on July 1, 1908, consisting of an estimated 2,224,091 acres {900,058.5 hectares} of pristine forestry. To the north is the Clearwater National Forest, established on July 1, 1908, and combined with the Nez Perce National Forest in 2012. To the west is the Wallowa-Whitman National Forest, a 2,392,508-acre {968,214.5-hectare} forest primarily located in Oregon, with a small section in Idaho. To the south is the Payette National Forest, which is the primary component of the Frank Church-River of No Return Wilderness {the second-largest designated wilderness in the United States} and the third-largest component of the Hells Canyon Wilderness.

6. In June 1985, due to extremely hot and arid weather, a swarm of grasshoppers devastated several western states. In Idaho, an estimated 1,800 insects per square yard {0.836 square meters} covered the land. The grasshoppers destroyed an estimated six million acres {2,428,113.853 hectares} of crops in Idaho, costing the state over $11 million {1985 USD} in damages.

7. There are three known types of caves in Idaho: Corrosion {formed from the erosive action of water, waves, or currents}, Solution {formed when acidic water seeps into cracks, dissolving the rocks it touches}, and Lava {formed after the eruption of a volcano}. The Shoshone Ice Caves is approximately 1,000 feet {304.8 meters} long and is a lava tube cave. The ice cave features an estimated 30 feet {9.144 meters} of ice encased in jagged lava

rock. The temperature inside the cave stays between 24 degrees Fahrenheit {-4.44 degrees Celsius} and 32 degrees Fahrenheit {0 degrees Celsius} year-round, causing the cave to remain permanently frozen.

8. The highest mountain in Idaho is Borah Peak. The mountain peak, commonly called "Mount Borah" or "Beauty Peak," has an elevation of approximately 12,662 feet {3,859.378 meters} and a prominence of approximately 5,982 feet {1,823.314 meters}. It is considered one of the most prominent peaks in the contiguous United States. Idaho's lowest elevation is located in Lewiston {Nez Perce County} at the confluence of the Snake and Clearwater Rivers, with an estimated elevation of 738 feet {224.942 meters} above sea level.

9. According to Nez Perce legend, seven giants lived in the Blue Mountains of eastern Oregon. Each year, the monsters would travel east, grabbing Nez Perce children who crossed their path. The Nez Perce tribal chief sought aid from the coyote to free the children. The coyote agreed to help and asked the fox for advice on how to handle the mighty giants. The fox told the coyote to dig seven very deep holes filled with boiling liquid. The coyote gathered all the animals with claws {cougars, bears, marmots, and beavers} to help dig the holes. After the holes were dug, the coyote filled them with a rust-colored liquid. Then, the coyote and the fox dropped hot rocks into the liquid to make it boil. The next time the giants traveled east, they fell into the seven deep holes of boiling liquid. Unable to escape, the coyote emerged and told the giants that because of their wickedness, they would become tall mountain peaks to remind everyone of their bad deeds. The coyote then changed the giants into the Seven Devils Mountains. Afterward, he struck the earth, opening a deep gash that created Hells Canyon at the feet of the petrified giants.

10. The heating system for Idaho's State Capitol Building is powered by a geothermal water basin located approximately

3,000 feet {914.4 meters} underground. To date, Idaho is the only state that uses a renewable source of energy for heating its Capitol building.

11. Bruneau Dunes State Park {Owyhee County} spans approximately 4,800 acres {1,942.491 hectares} and offers sandboarding, fishing, bird watching, and a public observatory. Located inside the park is North America's tallest single-structured dune, which stands approximately 470 feet {143.256 meters} high.

12. There are an estimated 72 gems found in Idaho, among which are star garnets. Star garnets form in specific geological areas, mainly in alluvial deposits. The Emerald Creek Garnet Area {St. Maries, Benewah County} allows visitors to mine for star garnets during the summer months {typically between Memorial Day weekend and Labor Day}. The only other known place in the world where star garnets are known to exist is India.

13. Idaho has 340 geothermal hot springs. Vulcan Hot Springs {Valley County} is considered one of the largest geothermal hot springs in Idaho. The hot spring is an estimated 30 feet {9.144 meters} across and features water temperatures around 192 degrees Fahrenheit {88.89 degrees Celsius}. Timber from the Boise National Forest was used in the creation of the emerald-green geothermal pool.

14. Since 2013, each year on January 1st at the stroke of midnight, citizens in Boise {Ada County}, have welcomed the new year by dropping a giant glowing potato using a crane. The event is commonly known as the Idaho Glowtato and is held at the Idaho State Captiol.

15. There are approximately 63 named waterfalls in Idaho. Goat Falls {Pierce County} is the tallest, with an elevation of approximately 8,100 feet {2,468.88 meters}, while Selway Falls

{Idaho County} is one of the smallest, with an elevation of approximately 1,700 feet {518.16 meters}.

16. Idaho has approximately 107,651 miles {173,247.491 kilometers} of rivers and an estimated 2,000 lakes. Lake Pend Oreille {Bonner and Kootenai Counties} is Idaho's largest lake, with a surface area of approximately 148 square miles {383.318 square kilometers} and a surface elevation of approximately 2,050 feet {624.84 meters}.

17. From Heaven's Gate Lookout {Idaho County}, you can see Washington, Montana, Oregon, and Idaho. Heaven's Gate Lookout is located at the entrance of the Seven Devils Mountains, high above Hells Canyon.

18. Contrary to its name, the Seven Devils Peaks {west-central Idaho} consist of 64 named peaks. The tallest is He Devil, with an elevation of approximately 9,400 feet {2,865.12 meters} and a prominence of approximately 5,200 feet {1,584.96 meters}.

19. On January 1, 1980, the River of No Return Wilderness was established. The act combined the Idaho Primitive Area, the Salmon River Breaks Primitive Area, and a portion of the Magruder Corridor. It also added approximately 125 miles {201.168 kilometers} of the Salmon River to the Wild and Scenic Rivers System. The wilderness covers an estimated 2,361,767 acres {955,770 hectares} and features several mountain ranges, six national forests, and the Salmon River. The River of No Return Wilderness is the second-largest wilderness area in the continental United States {Death Valley is the largest}. On March 14, 1984, the sitting U.S. President signed the act to rename the wilderness the Frank Church-River of No Return Wilderness {after a U.S. Senator born in Idaho}.

20. The geographic center of Idaho is located in Custer County, approximately 24 miles {38.62 kilometers} southwest of Challis,

RONDA SEXTON

## on the Yankee Fork River.

AMERICA THE BOLD, AMERICA THE BRAVE, AMERICA THE BEAUTIFUL

## What Was Idaho Thinking

## Ten Crazy Laws In Idaho

1. Yelling, hooting, whistling, or singing on or near public streets, which interfere with the comfort of property owners, is banned in Aberdeen.

2. Jefferson County requires all newly constructed buildings to be anchored.

3. In the city of Kuna, riding a horse at night requires a light equivalent to a 2-cell flashlight visible for a distance of 50 feet {15.24 meters} in front of and in the back of the horse.

4. The city of Homedale forbids the discharge or firing of BB guns.

5. The Idaho Constitution states, "To use a white or white-tipped with red cane {walking stick}, a person must be partially or wholly blind."

6. Eagle laws prohibit the sweeping of dirt {mainly leaves} into the street.

7. Soda Springs city ordinance bans anyone from operating {or permitting the operation} of any wire or wires for carrying energy, which causes interference with radio or television reception.

8. No piles of manure can be placed within the town of Notus.

9. Nez Perce County requires anyone requesting a license for alcoholic beverage sales to be the bona fide owner of such business.

10. A 1919 Idaho law forbids anyone from fishing while mounted on a horse.


****Please note, these laws may no longer be on the books; however, they were a law during some point in Idaho's history****

# Illinois

*"Illinois: a tapestry of endless horizons, where rolling fields, serene lakes, and vibrant forests weave together the essence of nature's quiet grace."*

CHATGPT {AI Generator}

RONDA SEXTON

## *Illinois Stats*

## Statehood:

Date Granted: December 3, 1818
Rank of Admission: Illinois became the 21st state to join the United States.

## State Capital:

Capital City: Springfield {Sangamon County}
Adopted date: February 25, 1837
Capitol Building Design Architect:
John C. Cochrane {Current Building}
George O. Garnsey {Current Building}
Alfred H. Piquenard {Current Building}
William Warren Boyington {Current Building}

## State Population:

Population: 12,812,508 {US Federal Census 2020}
Rank: 6th most populous in the United States

## Land Mass:

Total Land Mass: 56,343 square miles {145,927.700 square kilometers}
Rank: 25th in Rank of Largest State(s) in the United States

RONDA SEXTON

*Lovely Weather of Illinois*

### Record Highest Temperature:

Date: July 14, 1954
Location: East St. Louis {St. Clair County}
Temperature: 117 degrees Fahrenheit {47.22 degrees Celsius}

### Record Lowest Temperature:

Date: January 31, 2019
Location: Mount Carroll {Carroll County}
Temperature: -38 degrees Fahrenheit {-38.89 degrees Celsius}

### Record Snowfall:

Date: February 28, 1900
Location: Astoria {Fulton County}
Amount: 36.0 inches {91.44 centimeters} (within a 24-hour timeframe)

## Record Precipitation:

Date: July 18, 1996
Location: Aurora {DuPage County}
Amount: 16.91 inches {42.951 centimeters} (within a 24-hour timeframe)

## Major Earthquake:

Date: April 18, 2008
Location: Wabash County { 4 miles or 6.437 kilometers NNE of Bellmont}
Magnitude: 5.2 {Richter Scale}

AMERICA THE BOLD, AMERICA THE BRAVE, AMERICA THE BEAUTIFUL

## Illinois Pride

### State Name Origin:

Illinois derives from the French spelling of the Peoria Native American word "Iliniwok" meaning Men {Warriors}

### State Nickname(S):

Prairie State
Land of Lincoln
Garden of the West

### State Slogan:

The Prairie State

### State Motto:

State Sovereignty, National Union

AMERICA THE BOLD, AMERICA THE BRAVE, AMERICA THE BEAUTIFUL

# Symbols of Illinois

RONDA SEXTON

## State Bird:

Northern Cardinal
"Cardinalis cardinalis"
Adopted date: June 4, 1929

## State Flag:

Designed by: Replica of the Illinois State Seal
Adopted date: July 1, 1970

RONDA SEXTON

**State Flower:**

Native Violet
"Viola sororia"
Adopted date: January 21, 1908

**State Quarter:**

Released date: January 2, 2003
21st quarter released, honoring all 50 states
Themed: "The Land of Lincoln"
Highlights: Young Abraham Lincoln, Farmland, and Chicago skyline
Highlights: Young Abraham Lincoln, Farmland, and Chicago skyline
Designed by: Illinois school children sent various design concepts to a special committee. The concepts were narrowed down to three finalists, in which the Governor chose the winning design.
Engraved by: Donna Weaver

## State Song:

Illinois
Written by: Charles H. Chamberlain
Composed by: Archibald Johnston
Adopted date: June 30, 1925

**State Tree:**

Native Oak
"Quercus alba"
Adopted date: February 21, 1908

RONDA SEXTON

## Illinois Facts

## Twenty Interesting Facts About Illinois

1. On October 8, 1871, one of Illinois' largest fires started in a residential barn in Cook County {many dispute this}. The fire, commonly known as the Great Chicago Fire, burned approximately 17,000 buildings and caused an estimated $200 million {USD} in damage. The fire killed between 200 and 300 people and left over 100,000 people homeless. It lasted until October 10, 1871, with most residents attributing the spread of the fire to the massive number of wooden buildings and the dry weather.

2. A portion of Illinois' boundary is formed by three rivers: the Mississippi River {western border}, the Ohio River {southern border}, and the Wabash River {eastern border}.

3. In an attempt to prevent epidemics of water-borne diseases, mainly cholera, the flow of the Chicago River was reversed. The reversal took eight years to complete, with a workforce of over 8,000 laborers.

4. The geographical center of Illinois is located in Aetna Township {Logan County}, approximately 28 miles {45.062 kilometers} northeast of Springfield.

5. On February 10, 1996, the first National Tallgrass Prairie was established by the federal government. Midewin National Tallgrass Prairie is designed to preserve the native populations and habitats of fish, wildlife, and plants. The conservation site, located in Will County, covers an estimated 20,000 acres {8,093.713 hectares} of land.

6. Chicago gained its nickname, "The Windy City," in 1876. Many people are unsure whether the nickname refers to dirty

politicians or the breeze flowing off Lake Michigan.

7. Between the Mississippi River and the Ohio River lies the Shawnee National Forest. The forest covers approximately 265,616 acres {107,490.982 hectares}, spanning nine counties {Alexander, Jackson, Johnson, Gallatin, Hardin, Massac, Pope, Saline, and Union Counties}. The National Forest features an estimated 403-mile {648.57-kilometer} system of hiking trails, the Little Grand Canyon {a box canyon in Jackson County}, and the Garden of the Gods Wilderness. The Garden of the Gods Wilderness covers approximately 3,318 acres {1,342.747 hectares} in Gallatin, Pope, and Saline Counties. Within the wilderness is an estimated 0.5-mile {0.805-kilometer} trail that leads to an observation site featuring sandstone formations, providing viewers miles of spectacular views of southern Illinois and the forest.

8. The Willis Tower {formerly known as the Sears Tower} is a 110-story skyscraper located in Chicago {Cook County}. The tower opened on September 9, 1973, and stands at an estimated 1,454 feet {443.179 meters}. Several visitors claim that while standing on the Skydeck of the Willis Tower, they can see parts of Illinois, Indiana, Wisconsin, and Michigan.

9. On May 4, 1886, in Chicago {Cook County}, protesters demanded an eight-hour workday. After weeks of protesting, someone threw a bomb during a demonstration at Randolph Street Haymarket. The bomb killed eight officers and injured 60 people. The police arrested eight people without a clear identification of the bomber. The eight anarchists were tried and convicted of murder. The outcome of the trial led many to believe it was a grave miscarriage of justice.

10. Located in Jo Daviess County, Charles Mound is the highest natural point in Illinois. Charles Mound stands at approximately 1,235 feet {376.428 meters} above sea level and is considered

the lowest state high point in the Midwest {Illinois, Indiana, Iowa, Kansas, Michigan, Minnesota, Missouri, Nebraska, North Dakota, Ohio, South Dakota, and Wisconsin}.

11. Each year, in celebration of Saint Patrick's Day, the Chicago River is dyed green. The tradition began in 1962, and continue to date.

12. In 1881, the city of Aurora {Kane County} became the first town in Illinois to illuminate a city street with electric lights. The town placed light towers atop six buildings, illuminating the downtown area. Many citizens criticized the placement of the lights, stating that in certain areas the lights were bright enough to see your watch; however, if you walked a few feet away, you were in total darkness. To solve the issue, the town's residents donated $8,000 worth of lights featuring 14-foot {4.267-meter} tall light poles designed by the American Woodworking Company. Each pole carried three new tungsten light bulbs, which were promptly turned on for the first time at 7:00 p.m. {CDT} on November 21, 1908.

13. Around midnight on June 25, 1973, a couple was parked near a boat ramp on the Big Muddy River {Murphysboro, Jackson County}. They began hearing screams coming from the nearby woods. The couple looked toward the woods and saw a creature standing approximately 7 feet {2.134 meters} tall. The creature had light-colored fur matted with mud and glowing pink eyes. It began running toward the couple, causing them to quickly start their vehicle and leave the area. They went straight to the local police department and filed a report about what they had seen. Two officers arrived on the scene and recovered footprints, some measuring an estimated 12 inches {30.48 centimeters} long. The police officers began hearing the screams and splashing in the water. The splashes sounded like a large creature in the water; however, the officers never saw anything. The next night, a 4-year-old boy was playing in his backyard when he noticed

something nearby. He ran into the house, telling his parents he had seen a white ghost. Ten minutes later, the family's neighbor witnessed the creature while sitting on their back porch. Police soon arrived; however, the creature was not found. The last reported sighting of the Murphysboro Mud Monster was on July 7, 1973. No one is sure what the monster was or why it disappeared.

14. Carlyle Lake is the largest man-made lake in Illinois. The reservoir is approximately 15 miles {24.140 kilometers} long, an estimated 3.5 miles {5.633 kilometers} wide, and covers an estimated 26,000 acres {10,521.827 hectares}. The Kaskaskia River is the longest natural river in Illinois, measuring approximately 325 miles {523.037 kilometers}.

15. Out of the 102 counties in Illinois, only 18 counties were not named after famous American leaders. These counties include Champaign, Cumberland, DuPage, Iroquois, Jersey, Kankakee, Lake, Macoupin, Massac, Peoria, Richland, Rock Island, Saline, Sangamon, Union, Vermilion, Wabash, and Winnebago.

16. Illinois has more units of local government than any other state, including cities, counties, and towns. There are an estimated 6,963 local governments, with some counts as high as 8,923 in total.

17. Illinois is home to 309 state parks, covering an estimated 475,000 acres {192,225.68 hectares} of land. The largest state park is Pere Marquette State Park {Jersey County} with an estimated 8,050 acres {3,257.719 hectares}. William G. Stratton State Park {Grundy County} is the smallest, with an estimated 6.5 acres {2.630 hectares}.

18. The four stars on the Chicago flag represent four major events in Chicago's {Cook County} history. The first star represents the Chicago Fire, the 1871 fire that destroyed a

majority of the city. The second star represents the World's Columbian Exposition, the 1892 exposition honoring the arrival of Europeans. The third star represents the Century of Progress Exposition, the 1933 exposition emphasizing a perfect world through technology. The fourth star represents Fort Dearborn, a fort built in 1803 beside the Chicago River.

19. On October 21, 1892, the city of Chicago {Cook County} held an exposition in Jackson Park. The fair, commonly known as the World's Columbian Exposition or the Chicago World's Fair, was held in honor of the 400th anniversary of the European arrival in the New World. The fairgrounds later opened to the public on May 1, 1893, and closed on October 30, 1893. On October 9, 1893, the city of Chicago designated the date as Chicago Day, during which the fair set world records {to date} for outdoor attendance at 751,026 people.

20. There are an estimated 300 caves located in Illinois. Cave-in-Rock {Hardin County} is a state-owned cave open to the public year-round. The cave is approximately 55 feet {16.764 meters} wide and was formed during the 1811–1812 New Madrid earthquakes.

RONDA SEXTON

## What Was Illinois Thinking

## Ten Crazy Laws In Ilinois

1. In Chicago Heights, a beautician cannot practice beauty culture, for the purpose of treating a muscular or nervous disorder.

2. In Peoria, all yard waste must be placed in a 32-gallon {121.133 liters} bag {or less} and separated from other waste.

3. In the village of Crete, all bicycles must be registered with the chief of police within 30 days of purchase.

4. In the town of Alsip, it is illegal to overload, overdrive, or overwork any animal.

5. Des Plaines banned all pedestrians from standing on sidewalks, except when reasonably possible to the building line.

6. In Normal, residents are not allowed to keep an elephant, jaguar, bobcat, bear, or coyote in the city limits.

7. Singing loudly at a funeral site is illegal in Illinois.

8. Any homeowner who allows a weed to flower could face a fine in Forsyth.

9. In the village of Sleepy Hollow, no vehicles owned by a public entity or its servants are allowed on pleasure driveways.

10. In the town of Geneva, impersonating {without lawful authority} any city officer or employee is illegal.

****Please note, these laws may no longer be on the books; however, they were a law during some point in Illinois history****

# Indiana

RONDA SEXTON

*"Indiana's natural beauty is a hidden melody, where the rolling hills, peaceful forests, and tranquil rivers harmonize to create a quiet, enduring symphony of the heartland."*

CHATGPT {AI Generator}

AMERICA THE BOLD, AMERICA THE BRAVE, AMERICA THE BEAUTIFUL

# *Indiana Stats*

## Statehood:

Date Granted: December 11, 1816
Rank of Admission: Indiana became the 19th state to join the United States.

## State Capital:

Capital City: Indianapolis {Marion County}
Adopted date: January 6, 1821
Capitol Building Design Architect(s):
Edwin May {Current Building}
Adolph Scherrer {Current Building}

## State Population:

Population: 6,785,528 {US Federal Census 2020}
Rank: 17th most populous in the United States

## Land Mass:

Total Land Mass: 36,185 square miles {93,718.720 square kilometers}
Rank: 38th in Rank of Largest State(s) in the United States

AMERICA THE BOLD, AMERICA THE BRAVE, AMERICA THE BEAUTIFUL

*Lovely Weather of Indiana*

## Record Highest Temperature:

Date: July 14, 1936
Location: Collegeville {Jasper County}
Temperature: 116 degrees Fahrenheit {46.67 degrees Celsius}

## Record Lowest Temperature:

Date: January 19, 1994
Location: New Whiteland {Johnson County}
Temperature: -36 degrees Fahrenheit {-37.78 degrees Celsius}

## Record Snowfall:

Date: December 23, 2004
Location: Salem {Washington County}
Amount: 33.0 inches {83.82 centimeters} (within a 24-hour timeframe)

### Record Precipitation:

Date: August 6, 1905
Location: Princeton {Gibson County}
Amount: 10.5 inches {26.67 centimeters} (within a 24-hour timeframe)

### Major Earthquake:

Date: September 27, 1909
Location: Parke County {2.5 miles or 4.023 Kilometers NNE of Rockville}
Magnitude: 5.1 {Richter Scale}

RONDA SEXTON

*Indiana Pride*

### State Name Origin:

Indiana is in honor of the Native Americans, meaning "Land Of The Indians" {Indian Land}

### State Nickname(S):

The Hoosier State
Mr. Hoosier
The Indiana Historian

### State Slogan:

The Hoosier State

### State Motto:

The Crossroads Of America

RONDA SEXTON

# Symbols of Indiana

**State Bird:**

Cardinal
"Cardinalis cardinalis"
Adopted date: March 2, 1933

RONDA SEXTON

## State Flag:

Designed by: Paul Hadley
Adopted date: May 31, 1917

**State Flower:**

Peony
"Paeonia"
Adopted date: March 15, 1957

**State Quarter:**

Release date: August 8, 2002
19th quarter released, honoring all 50 states
Themed: Crossroads of America
Highlights: Indy race car, and the outline of the state of Indiana
Designed by: Josh Harvey
Engraved by: Donna Weaver

**State Song:**

On the Banks of the Wabash, Far Away
Written by: Paul Dresser
Composed by: Paul Dresser
Adopted date: March 14, 1913

RONDA SEXTON

**State Tree:**

Tulip Tree
"Liriodendron Tulipifera"
Adopted date: March 3, 1931

## Indiana Facts

## Twenty Interesting Facts About Indiana

1. On May 30, 1911, the first long-distance auto race was held in Indianapolis {Marion County}. The race consists of 200 laps {approximately 500 miles or 804.67 kilometers} and is held every Memorial Day weekend. The first winner's average speed was 75 mph {120.7 km/h}, with a winning prize of $14,000 {1911 USD}. The 106th annual race was held on May 29, 2022. The winner had an average speed of 175.428 mph {282.32 km/h} and a winning prize of $3.1 million {2022 USD}.

2. Hoosier Hill {Wayne County} is the highest natural point in Indiana. The hill has an elevation of approximately 1,257 feet {383.13 meters} above sea level, featuring a prominence of approximately 297 feet {90.53 meters}. Indiana's lowest natural point is located in Posey County, where the Wabash River and the Ohio River meet. This point has an elevation of approximately 320 feet {97.54 meters} above sea level.

3. Bluespring Caverns {Lawrence County} features the longest underground river discovered in the United States. The cave system stretches approximately 20 miles {32.19 kilometers} of surveyed passages and includes an estimated 15-acre {6.07-hectare} sinkhole.

4. Santa Claus {Spencer County} was originally named Santa Fe. In 1856, the town established a post office; however, the Post Office Department refused the application, citing another town was already named Santa Fe in Miami County. The residents hosted a town meeting where the name "Santa Claus" was selected. Today, the town receives an estimated 20,000 letters during the Christmas season, all of which are read and replied to. On August 3, 1946, the first theme park in the United States was built in Santa Claus and is still open to the public.

5. There are approximately 100 lakes in Indiana. Lake Wawasee {Kosciusko County}, formerly known as Turkey Lake, is Indiana's largest natural lake, with an average depth of approximately 22 feet {6.71 meters} and a maximum depth of 77 feet {23.47 meters}. Tippecanoe Lake {Kosciusko County} is the deepest natural lake in Indiana, with an average depth of approximately 37 feet {11.28 meters} and a maximum depth of approximately 121 feet {36.88 meters}. Lake Monroe {Monroe County} is the largest man-made lake, covering an estimated 10,750 acres {4,350.37 hectares} with a maximum depth of approximately 59 feet {17.98 meters}.

6. Indiana has the shortest shoreline of any Great Lakes state in the United States. The state shares a coastline with Lake Michigan that is approximately 45 miles {72.42 kilometers} long. Despite the short shoreline, Indiana is still considered a "Great Lakes State."

7. On October 6, 1866, the first train robbery occurred in Jackson County, Indiana. Robberies had occurred prior {on stationary trains sitting in depots or freight yards}; however, two brothers managed to stop a moving train in a remote area, taking an estimated $13,000 from the train crew and passengers. This new method of robbing trains quickly became popular across the West, due to sparsely populated areas. Several criminal gangs found train robbery easy and lucrative, making it their criminal specialty.

8. The Maumee River is the only river in Indiana that flows north and east into Lake Erie. It is also the largest watershed {drainage basin} of any Great Lakes river. The watershed is divided into nine separate sub-basins, covering an estimated 6,919 square miles {17,920.13 square kilometers}.

9. On March 31, 1880, the Wabash County Courthouse lit four

3,000-candlepower lamps in the dome of the courthouse. The lamps were lit at approximately 8 p.m. and could be seen from approximately 1 mile {1.61 kilometers} away. This was the first time a building was lit by electricity in Indiana {some claim in the world}.

10. On June 22, 1918, a Michigan Central troop train engineer was traveling toward Hammond {Lake County}. Near Hammond, a slow-moving train used by the Hagenbeck-Wallace Circus had been moved to a siding to fix a mechanical problem, leaving some wooden cars on the mainline track. At approximately 4 a.m., the Michigan Central engineer missed several automatic signals and warnings posted by the circus train's brakeman. The troop train collided with the circus train, causing a lamp {used to illuminate the cars} to ignite the wooden cars, resulting in a fire to quickly spread. The wreck killed 86 people and injured another 127. To this day, the wreck is considered one of the deadliest train disasters in United States history.

11. On January 31, 1971, Apollo 14 made a lunar trip to the moon. A former U.S. Forest Service smokejumper {an experienced wildland firefighter} was aboard the rocket, carrying hundreds of tree seeds as part of a joint NASA/USFS project. Once the smokejumper returned to Earth, the seeds were germinated by the Forest Service and planted in several locations across America. Among the trees, commonly known as "Moon Trees", is a sycamore planted at Camp Koch Girl Scout Camp in Cannelton {Perry County}. The Indianapolis Statehouse {Marion County} is home to the second sycamore Moon Tree. Lincoln State Park {Spencer County} features a third sycamore Moon Tree. Additionally, Tell City {Perry County} has two sweetgum Moon Trees planted at the Forest Service Office.

12. There are approximately 2,902 caves discovered in Indiana. Indiana Caverns {Harrison County} is the longest cave in the

state. Development began on June 1, 2012, and the cave opened to the public on June 15, 2013. By the end of 2015, the cave measured approximately 42.57 miles {68.51 kilometers} in surveyed length, with about 10 miles {16.09 kilometers} of passageways left undiscovered.

13. Beginning in 1888, a memorial monument to honor Civil War veterans {later dedicated to all Indiana military members} was erected in Indianapolis {Marion County}. In 1893, the World's Columbian Exhibition in Chicago {Cook County} delayed construction. The monument was completed in 1901 and dedicated on May 15, 1902. Over time, the Soldiers and Sailors Monument began to lose its prestige. To renew public interest, the monument is now decorated each Christmas as a large Christmas tree. The monument stands approximately 284.6 feet {86.75 meters} tall and is adorned with 52 strands of garland and approximately 4,784 lights. On February 13, 1973, the monument was added to the National Register of Historic Places.

14. Indiana is divided into several natural regions. Northern Indiana is mainly flat to rolling terrain, with hundreds of kettle lakes in some areas. Northwest Indiana features various sand ridges and dunes. Central Indiana is primarily flat, with some rolling hills and shallow valleys. The southern portion of the state consists of rugged, hilly terrain with many valleys, caves, caverns, and quarries.

15. On March 18, 1925, a string of tornadoes traveled through Missouri, Indiana, and Illinois. Commonly known as the "Tri-State Tornado," the storm is considered one of the deadliest tornado events in American history. The vortex produced an estimated 12 tornadoes, lasting approximately seven hours and covering an estimated 219 miles {352.45 kilometers}. When it entered Indiana, the vortex was approximately 0.75 miles {1.21 kilometers} wide and destroyed 150 homes and 85 farms before

dissipating in Pike County, Indiana. In total, the tornadoes caused an estimated $2.4 billion {2021 USD} in damages, injuring approximately 2,027 people and killing 695 {71 deaths in Indiana}.

16. Indiana was once a leading vehicle manufacturing state. In 1909, it ranked second in car production {after Henry Ford's Michigan plant}. By 1919, the state was home to 172 car manufacturers, including Auburn, Cole, Cord, Duesenberg, Marmon, and Studebaker Brothers. Due to the Great Depression, World Wars I and II, labor market changes, and mass production by GM, Ford, and Chrysler, many car companies were forced to cease production or file for bankruptcy.

17. There are three national parks in Indiana. The Lincoln Boyhood National Memorial, approved by Congress in 1962, features the childhood home of a former president and covers approximately 200 acres {80.94 hectares} in Spencer County. The George Rogers Clark National Historical Park, approved on July 23, 1966, features a bronze statue of an American Revolutionary hero and covers approximately 24.3 acres {9.83 hectares} in Knox County. The Indiana Dunes National Park, approved by Congress in 2019, runs approximately 20 miles {32.19 kilometers} along the southern shore of Lake Michigan and covers an estimated 15,067 acres {6,097.40 hectares}. Located in Porter, Lake, and LaPorte counties, the park features Pinhook Bog, the Heron Rookery, the Calumet Prairie State Nature Preserve, and the Hobart Prairie Grove.

18. Between Monroe County and Lawrence County lies a vast deposit of top-grade limestone. In 1928, an estimated 18,630 tons {16,900,850 kilograms} of limestone were quarried from the Empire Quarry {Monroe County} to build the Empire State Building in New York City. Today, the limestone quarries still produce up to an estimated 2 million cubic feet {56,633.69 cubic meters} of limestone each year.

19. Approximately 1.5 miles {2.41 kilometers} north of SR 334, a marker was erected by the Indiana Sesquicentennial Commission in 1966, stating that the geographical center of Indiana is located in Boone County. However, the true geographical center is known to be approximately 14 miles {22.53 kilometers} north-northwest of Indianapolis {Marion County}.

20. A very successful businessman was deeply afraid of being buried alive. His final wish was for his family to install a telephone inside his mausoleum in case his worst fear came true. Upon his death, his family honored his wishes and installed the phone inside the tomb. Years later, the man's widow passed away. When her body was discovered, she was holding the phone receiver in her hand. Many believe she was trying to call for help before her passing. When the mausoleum was opened to place her in her final resting place, the phone receiver {installed in the tomb} was found off the hook.

RONDA SEXTON

# What Was Indiana Thinking

## Ten Crazy Laws In Indiana

1. To see a hypnotist, a current patient {who had a past relationship with the hypnotist} must wait five years after the relationship ends to request medical services.

2. South Bend bans all peddlers from crying in order to maintain the peace and quiet of the neighborhood.

3. It is unlawful to catch fish by the means of using a net or trap.

4. All horse-drawn carriages are banned Monday-Friday after 6:00 p.m. on any Indianapolis public streets.

5. Noble County prohibits any individual under the age of 14 {with or without parental consent} from receiving a body piercing procedure performed by an individual under the age of 16.

6. In Warsaw, you cannot throw any hard substance or missile across {or over} any street, alley, or sidewalk.

7. In Wabash, all drains {gutters} that are unclean or damaged are considered a public nuisance.

8. In Beech Grove, ice cream trucks are banned within residential neighborhoods, public streets, public right of way, and easements.

9. Wanatah bans anyone from annoying {teasing} any dog or cat.

10. All cul-de-sacs located in the city of Merrillville must have a landscaped island no larger than 66 feet {20.117 meters} in diameter.


****Please note, these laws may no longer be on the books; however, they were a law during some point in Indiana's history****

# Iowa

RONDA SEXTON

*"Iowa's beauty is found in the gentle sway of golden fields, the calm embrace of winding rivers, and the vast skies that stretch endlessly over the heart of the Midwest."*

CHATGPT {AI Generator}

AMERICA THE BOLD, AMERICA THE BRAVE, AMERICA THE BEAUTIFUL

## Iowa Stats

## Statehood:

Date Granted: December 28, 1846
Rank of Admission: Iowa became the 29th state to join the United States.

## State Capital:

Capital City: Des Moines {Polk County}
Adopted date: September 3, 1857
Capitol Building Design Architect(s):
John C. Cochrane {Current Building}
Alfred H. Piquenard {Current Building}
Mifflin E. Bell {Current Building}
William F. Hackney {Current Building}

## State Population:

Population: 3,190,369 {US Federal Census 2020}
Rank: 31st most populous in the United States

## Land Mass:

Total Land Mass: 56,276 square miles {145,754.17 square kilometers}
Rank: 26th in Rank of The Largest State(s) in the United States

AMERICA THE BOLD, AMERICA THE BRAVE, AMERICA THE BEAUTIFUL

## Lovely Weather of Iowa

## Record Highest Temperature:

Date: July 20, 1934
Location: Keokuk {Lee County}
Temperature: 118 degrees Fahrenheit {47.78 degrees Celsius}

## Record Lowest Temperature:

Date: February 3, 1996
Location: Elkader {Clayton County}
Temperature: -47 degrees Fahrenheit {-43.89 degrees Celsius}

## Record Lowest Temperature:

Date: January 12, 1912
Location: Washta {Cherokee County}
Temperature: -47 degrees Fahrenheit {-43.89 degrees Celsius}

### Record Snowfall:

Date: April 20, 1918
Location: Lenox {Taylor County}
Amount: 24.0 inches {60.96 centimeters} (within a 24-hour timeframe)

### Record Precipitation:

Date: June 14, 1998
Location: Atlantic {Cass County}
Amount: 13.18 inches {33.477 centimeters} (within a 24-hour time frame)

### Major Earthquake:

Date: April 13, 1905
Location: Lee County {near Keokuk}
Magnitude: 4.0 {Richter Scale}

RONDA SEXTON

*Iowa Pride*

### State Name Origin:

Iowa derives from the French term "Ioway" for the Bah-kho-je Native Indian word "Ayuxwa" meaning "One who puts to sleep"

### State Nickname(S):

The Hawkeye State
The Corn State
Land of the Rolling Prairie

### State Slogan:

The Hawkeye State

### State Motto:

Our Liberties We Prize, And Our Rights We Will Maintain

RONDA SEXTON

*Symbols of Iowa*

**State Bird:**

American Goldfinch
"Carduelis tristis"
Adopted date: March 22, 1933

RONDA SEXTON

### State Flag:

Designed by: Dixie Cornell Gebhardt
Adopted date: March 29, 1921

**State Flower:**

Wild Prairie Rose
"Rosa arkansana"
Adopted date: May 7, 1897

**State Quarter:**

Released date: August 30, 2004
29th quarter released, honoring all 50 states
Themed: Foundation in Education
Highlights: One-room schoolhouse {inspired by the painting Arbor Day by Grant Wood}
Designed by: John Mercanti
Engraved by: John Mercanti

**State Song:**

"Song of Iowa"
Written by: Samuel Hawkins Marshall Myers
Composed by: N/A ***lyrics are sung to the music of Tannenbaum***
Adopted date: March 20, 1911

RONDA SEXTON

## State Tree:

Bur Oak
"Quercus macrocarpa"
Adopted date: March 13, 1961

AMERICA THE BOLD, AMERICA THE BRAVE, AMERICA THE BEAUTIFUL

# Iowa Facts

## Twenty Interesting Facts About Iowa

1. Located in Burlington {Des Moines County} is the most crooked street in America. The street lies between Columbia Street and Washington Street, covering an estimated 275 feet {83.8 meters} and rising approximately 58.3 feet {17.8 meters}. It is constructed of limestone and blue clay brick. The street, known as Burlington's Snake Alley, was featured by Ripley's Believe It or Not as the most crooked street in America.

2. Iowa and Missouri began a battle over a 12-mile {19.312-kilometer} strip of land bordering both states. When Missouri became a state, the border separating the two states was unclear to locals. The original treaty referred to the Des Moines Rapids {a section of the Mississippi River} as the endpoint of the borderline. However, one surveyor granted the State of Missouri 2,616 square miles {6,775.409 square kilometers} of land originally allocated to Iowa. In July 1839, a Missouri sheriff, believing the land belonged to Missouri, sent tax collectors to the disputed area. Citizens living there believed they resided in Iowa and began complaining to Iowa's governor. In October 1839, the Missouri sheriff attempted to collect taxes in the area but was forced back to Missouri under threat of violence from local residents. In retaliation, Missouri supporters cut down four trees that Iowa farmers had used as storehouses for honey bees. The sheriff returned to the disputed area and was arrested and jailed for "Usurpation of Authority." Both states mobilized militias and gathered troops along the disputed border. The conflict, commonly known as the Honey War, is one of the most unusual disputes over state boundaries. The disagreement was ultimately settled by the U.S. Supreme Court, which placed the border near its original location.

3. Iowa is home to 33 natural lakes. West Okoboji Lake

{Dickinson County} is Iowa's deepest natural lake, covering approximately 3,789 acres {1,533.354 hectares}, with a depth of approximately 135 feet {41.148 meters}. East Okoboji Lake {Dickinson County} is the longest natural lake in the state, stretching approximately 16 miles {25.75 kilometers}. Rathbun Dam and Reservoir, reaching approximately 21 miles {33.8 kilometers}, covers an estimated 21,000 acres {8,498.399 hectares}, and is the largest man-made body of water in Iowa. Iowa's largest glacier-made lake is Spirit Lake {Dickinson County}, covering an estimated 8.88 square miles {23 square kilometers} and ranking as the fourth-largest lake {natural or man-made} in Iowa.

4. Inaugurated on August 26, 1973, the Register's Annual Great Bicycle Ride Across Iowa is a non-competitive bicycle ride organized by The Des Moines Register. The ride, commonly known as RAGBRAI, changes its starting and ending locations each year. The 2021 course began in Le Mars {Plymouth County} and ended in Clinton {Clinton County}, with stops in Sac City {Sac County}, Fort Dodge {Webster County}, Iowa Falls {Hardin County}, Waterloo {Black Hawk County}, Anamosa {Jones County}, and DeWitt {Clinton County}. Throughout RAGBRAI's history, the ride has passed through all 99 of Iowa's counties, and 14 communities have served as starting points.

5. The Cowboy Breakfast Festival is an annual event held in September in Brandon {Buchanan County}. To honor the occasion, Brandon residents built a frying pan measuring approximately 9 feet {2.743 meters} wide and 14 feet {4.267 meters} long. The pan, constructed from scrap steel donated by local farmers, was used in 2004 to fry 44 dozen eggs and approximately 88 pounds {39.92 kilograms} of bacon. It is the largest frying pan in Iowa to date.

6. According to Kiowa Native American legend, seven girls from the Kiowa tribe wandered away from their camp to pick berries.

As they roamed around, several grizzly bears began watching them. Soon afterwards the bears began chasing the girls, causing them to climb a large rock. After sitting on the rock for a while, the bears remained underneath, causing the girls to cry out in desperation to the Great Spirit. Hearing their cries, the Great Spirit caused the rock to grow. The girls climbed higher to escape the bears, until they reached the sky. Many people believe that a small cluster of seven stars, which rises above Bear Lodge, represents the spirits of the seven girls.

7. There are an estimated 1,000 caves in Iowa. Coldwater Cave {Winneshiek County} is renowned as the longest cave, with an estimated 16 miles {25.75 kilometers} of documented passageways. Crystal Lake Cave {Dubuque County} is considered the largest show cave. Coachlight Caves {Des Moines County} are among the largest salt caves in the state. Inside Ice Cave {Decorah County}, temperatures remain around freezing for most of the year, causing ice deposits to linger on the cave walls until late summer. Ice Cave was listed on the National Register of Historic Places on December 20, 1978.

8. Iowa is home to 63 state parks and five state forests. Lake Macbride State Park {Johnson County} is the largest state park, covering 2,180 acres {882.215 hectares}. The park is divided into two units centered around Lake Macbride. The largest forest is Stephens State Forest, which covers an estimated 15,500 acres {6,272.628 hectares} across five counties {Lucas, Clarke, Monroe, Appanoose, and Davis}.

9. Located in West Bend {Kossuth and Palo Alto Counties} is a religious shrine known as the Grotto of the Redemption. The shrine consists of nine grottoes {natural or artificial caves} depicting scenes from the life of Jesus Christ. It is considered the world's most complete man-made collection of minerals, fossils, shells, and petrification located in one place {unofficially}. The estimated value of the rocks and minerals is $4.3 million, and

approximately 100,000 people visit the shrine annually. On February 23, 2001, the shrine was added to the U.S. National Register of Historic Places.

10. The state's highest point is Hawkeye Point {Osceola County}, with an elevation of approximately 1,670 feet {509.016 meters}. The lowest point is approximately 480 feet {146.304 meters} above sea level at Keokuk {Lee County}.

11. Since 1871, an estimated eleven F5 {EF5} tornadoes have been recorded in Iowa. On May 15, 1968, an F5 tornado struck Charles City {Floyd County}, injuring 462 people, killing 13, and causing an estimated $30 million {USD} in damages. On the same day, a second F5 tornado touched down in Fayette County, causing five additional fatalities, injuring 156 people, and destroying approximately 1,000 homes. It was the only time {to date} that Iowa experienced two F5 tornadoes on the same day.

12. Iowa is the only state bordered by two navigable rivers: the Mississippi River forms most of Iowa's eastern border, and the Missouri River forms most of its western border.

13. Iowa has a total of 28 named mountains. The tallest mountain is Hawkeye Point {Osceola County}, which rises to approximately 1,670 feet {509.016 meters} and a prominence of approximately 40 feet {12.192 meters}. Pilot Knob {Winnebago County} is an isolated, cone-shaped hill rising approximately 250 feet {76.2 meters} above the surrounding terrain. Pilot Knob is the most prominent hill in Iowa, with an estimated prominence of 325 feet {99.06 meters}.

14. Iowa has 99 counties and 100 county seats. Clarion {Wright County} is the only county seat located precisely at the center of its county. Lee County has two county seats: Fort Madison and Keokuk.

15. On August 4, 1862, the United States presidential administration mandated that each Union state provide approximately 300,000 militiamen for nine months of service or, alternatively, offer three-year enlistments with a reduced number of recruits. In Iowa, an estimated 76,242 men joined the Union Army for three-year enlistments. Although no battles were fought on Iowa soil, an estimated 11,000 Iowans were wounded during the American Civil War, approximately 3,000 died {primarily from sickness and disease}, and 28 received the Medal of Honor.

16. On December 15, 2021, Iowa was struck by a widespread, long-lived, straight-line windstorm known as a derecho. It was the first derecho storm to occur in December in United States history.

17. The first six-passenger electric wagons were developed in Des Moines {Polk County} in 1891. The wagons had a top speed of 14 MPH {23 km/h} and and was featured at the 1893 World's Columbian Exposition in Chicago {Cook County, Illinois}. By 1897, New York City {New York County, New York} had the first twelve electric city cabs. An estimated 38,842 electric cars were sold in the United States by 1912, however, by 1935, electric cars had virtually disappeared from the market. Over the years, several companies have continued to refine the concept of the electric car, improving electric batteries, speed, and vehicle range.

18. Sabula {Jackson County} is Iowa's only town located on an island. It is also the northern terminus {the final point} of US Route 67, an estimated 1,560 miles {2,510.577 kilometers} north-south highway located in central United States. Sabula covers approximately 1.46 square miles {3.781 square kilometers}, and according to the 2020 US Federal Census, the town's population is 506 residents. The southern terminus of

U.S. Route 67 is located in Presidio {Presidio County}, Texas.

19. Located in McGregor {Clayton County} at the base of a 90-foot {27.432-meter} bluff is a small, dark cave. In 1953, a local resident began blasting into the bluff and soon discovered a sizable cave with flowing water inside. He later blasted a separate work entrance into the side of the ravine and built a ramp leading into the cave. Commonly known as Spook Cave, the cave was opened to tourists in 1955 and remains the only underground boat tour in Iowa to date.

20. On August 21, 1814, the only international conflict ever to occur in Iowa took place over fur trade on the Mississippi River. The battle occurred on Credit Island, near Davenport {Scott County}. British troops, aided by the British Band {a group of Native Americans led by Black Hawk}, fought against US forces. The US military lost the conflict but later defeated the British Band during the Black Hawk War in the spring of 1832.

RONDA SEXTON

# What Was Iowa Thinking

## Ten Crazy Laws In Iowa

1. In Ottumwa, homeowners cannot use barbed wire to construct any fence.

2. Tying a floating device to a city wharf for more than 24 hours is a misdemeanor in Keokuk.

3. The city of Mount Vernon bans anyone from picking a flower in the city park.

4. The Iowa Constitution requires all hop growers to use 36 inches {91.44 centimeters}, 18 inches {45.72 centimeters} wide, and 23.25 inches {59.055 centimeters} deep standard box for packing hops.

5. The city of Algona forbids anyone from crying "fire" in the event there is no fire.

6. Ringing bells is a form of disturbing the peace and is prohibited in the city of Wilton.

7. In the city of Decorah, cows and horses are considered bothersome animals.

8. Alarming a person is considered harassment in Ottumwa and is against the law.

9. In Cedar Rapids, placing an item near a tree located in a public place is illegal {unless the City Forester permits it beforehand}.

10. While working in an amusement park in Des Moines, a guide or a scene character must carry an operable flashlight powered by a minimum of two C-cell batteries.

****Please note, these laws may no longer be on the books; however, they were a law during some point in Iowa's history****

# Kansas

RONDA SEXTON

> *"Kansas: a canvas painted with endless prairies, golden sunsets, and wide-open skies, where the beauty of the land stretches as far as the soul can see."*

CHATGPT {AI Generator}

AMERICA THE BOLD, AMERICA THE BRAVE, AMERICA THE BEAUTIFUL

# Kansas Stats

## Statehood:

Date Granted: January 29, 1861
Rank of Admission: Kansas became the 34th state to join the United States.

## State Capital:

Capital City: Topeka {Shawnee County}
Adopted date: July 29, 1859
Capitol Building Design Architect(s):
Edward Townsend Mix {Current Building}
John G. Haskell {Current Building}

## State Population:

Population: 2,937,880 {US Federal Census 2020}
Rank: 35th most populous in the United States

## Land Mass:

Total Land Mass: 82,282 square miles {213,109.40 square kilometers}
Rank: 15th in Rank of Largest State(s) in the United States

AMERICA THE BOLD, AMERICA THE BRAVE, AMERICA THE BEAUTIFUL

## Lovely Weather of Kansas

### Record Highest Temperature:

Date: July 24, 1936
Location: Alton {Osborne County}
Temperature: 121 degrees Fahrenheit {49.44 degrees Celsius}

### Record Highest Temperature:

Date: July 18, 1936
Location: Fredonia {Wilson County}
Temperature: 121 degrees Fahrenheit {49.44 degrees Celsius}

### Record Lowest Temperature:

Date: February 13, 1905
Location: Lebanon {Smith County}
Temperature: -40 degrees Fahrenheit {-40 degrees Celsius}

## Record Snowfall:

Date: March 28, 2009
Location: Pratt {Pratt County}
Amount: 30.0 inches {76.2 centimeters} (within a 24-hour timeframe)

## Record Precipitation:

Date: N/A
Location: N/A
Amount: N/A (within a 24-hour timeframe)

\*\*\* The National Oceanographic and Atmospheric Administration (NOAA) does not track precipitation in Kansas.

## Major Earthquake:

Date: April 24, 1867
Location: Manhattan {Riley County}
Magnitude: 5.1 {Richter Scale}

RONDA SEXTON

*Kansas Pride*

### State Name Origin:

Kansas derives from a French term of the Kaw Native American word "KaNze" meaning "South Wind"

### State Nickname(S):

The Sunflower State
The Jayhawk State
Midway, U.S.A.

### State Slogan(S):

The Sunflower State

### State Motto:

"Ad Astra Per Aspera" {To The Stars Through Difficulties}

RONDA SEXTON

*Symbols of Kansas*

## State Bird:

Western Meadowlark
"Sturnella Neglecta"
Adopted date: June 30, 1937

## State Flag:

Designed by: Hazel Avery
Adopted date: March 23, 1927
Revised date: September 24, 1961

**State Flower:**

Native Wild Sunflower
"Helianthus Annuus"
Adopted date: March 12, 1903

**State Quarter:**

Release date: August 29, 2005
34th quarter released, honoring all 50 states
Themed: N/A
Highlights: Sunflower motif and a buffalo
Designed by: Norman E. Nemeth
Engraved by: Norman E. Nemeth

**State Song:**

Home on the Range
Written by: Dr. Brewster M. Higley, VI
Composed by: Daniel E. Kelley
Adopted date: June 30, 1947

RONDA SEXTON

**State Tree:**

Cottonwood
"Populus Deltoides"
Adopted date: March 23, 1937

AMERICA THE BOLD, AMERICA THE BRAVE, AMERICA THE BEAUTIFUL

## Kansas Facts

## Twenty Interesting Facts About Kansas

1. The Red Hills are famous for their color. The hills are located in the southern and central sections of Kansas {primarily in Clark, Comanche, and Barber counties} and get their distinctive color from iron oxide {rust}. Approximately 350 of the 700 caves in the state are located in the Red Hills. Comanche County has approximately 128 caves, and Barber County features approximately 117. The caves are mainly composed of gypsum {a soft mineral commonly used in manufacturing blackboards, sidewalk chalk, and drywall} and average between approximately 100 and 300 feet {30.48 to 91.44 meters} in length.

2. Outside of mountainous areas, Dodge City {Ford County} is the windiest city in the United States, with an average wind speed of 14 MPH {22.53 km/h}.

3. Smith County {approximately 2 miles or 3.22 kilometers northwest of Lebanon} is the geographical center of the 48 contiguous states. On June 29, 1941, a monument was erected to mark the location. At the time, Alaska and Hawaii were not part of the United States. Afterward, the geographic center moved to Castle Rock {Butte County}, South Dakota.

4. Kansas is home to one of Hollywood's most successful movies. In the 1900s, a book series began with the first book titled The Wonderful Wizard of Oz. The author wrote fifteen full-length Oz books, and after his death, the publisher continued the series with nineteen more books. In 1922, an additional seven books {written by a different author} were added to the series, bringing the total to forty books. On August 25, 1939, a movie {based on the book series} began production in Hollywood. The production became a major Hollywood hit and is still enjoyed by many fans

today.

5. In White Cloud {Doniphan County}, you can see Iowa, Nebraska, Missouri, and Kansas while standing in one spot.

6. In July 1874, a grasshopper plague swarmed the state of Kansas. Many residents stated the swarms were so large that the grasshoppers blocked the sun, and the sound of their legs against their wings sounded like a rainstorm. During the plague, The First United Methodist Church in Hutchinson {Reno County} began constructing the church foundation. The pastor decided that instead of halting construction until after the plague, they would continue working. This decision resulted in thousands of grasshoppers being mixed into the mortar of the original building foundation.

7. In 1948, Kanopolis {Ellsworth County} became the first state park in Kansas. The park features Horsethief Canyon {sandstone bluffs}, Faris Caves {a series of artificially excavated caves}, the Smoky Hill Wildlife Area, and approximately 25 miles {40.23 kilometers} of hiking trails.

8. Commonly referred to as Tornado Alley, Kansas ranks second nationally in the average number of tornadoes per year {Texas ranks first with an average of 155 per year}. On average, approximately 96 tornadoes occur each year, most between April and June. According to the National Climatic Data Center {NCDC}, since 1950, there have only been seven years when Kansas did not report an EF3 or stronger tornado {1963, 1979, 1987, 1988, 1994, 1997, and 2006}. Scientists estimate that tornadoes typically only strike the same place once every 250 years. However, Codell {Rooks County} experienced three tornadoes on the same day for three consecutive years {May 20, 1916, May 20, 1917, and May 20, 1918}. On May 4, 2007, an F5 tornado struck Greensburg {Kiowa County}. The tornado lasted for approximately one hour and five minutes, killed 10

people, injured 60 others, and destroyed 95 percent of the city. According to the Enhanced Fujita scale, this was the first F5 tornado to form since May 3, 1999, in Moore {Cleveland County}, Oklahoma.

9. The Arkansas River runs through four states and is the sixth longest river in the United States. In Oklahoma, Colorado, and Arkansas, the river is pronounced "Arkansaw." In Kansas, it is pronounced "Ar-KAN-zuhs."

10. During the 1800s, the United States passed the Homestead Act of 1862, allowing people from other countries the opportunity to own land in exchange for five years of hard work and land improvements. A man, along with his wife and two children, took the opportunity and settled on a piece of land in Labette County, Kansas. In 1871, the family turned their homestead into a small inn and grocery store for people traveling on the Osage Trail. In May 1871, a man's body was found in a nearby creek. No one knew the man's identity or the circumstances that led to his violent death. Over the following months, several people reported missing relatives from Fort Scott {Bourbon County} and Independence {Montgomery County}. By 1873, rumors regarding missing people continued to circulate. Many citizens suspected the family's involvement; however, no evidence ever linked them to the crimes. Eventually, the family's neighbor stopped by their home to discuss some wandering cattle. He noticed the house was empty and appeared abandoned. Word spread throughout the town, and within days, the bodies of several missing people {including a three-year-old girl} were found on the farm. Several people reported sightings of the family in Colorado, Utah, Texas, Idaho, and Old Mexico. Many believe the family changed their name and began a killing spree in the Oklahoma Panhandle in August 1887.

11. The Big Basin Prairie Preserve covers approximately 1,818

acres {735.72 hectares}. The preserve {Clark County} features St. Jacob's Well {an estimated 58-foot or 17.68-meter-deep sinkhole} and the Big Basin {an estimated 100-foot or 30.48-meter-deep sinkhole}.

12. On November 9, 1888, a few minutes past 5 p.m., an explosion occurred in a mine shaft in Frontenac {Crawford County}. The explosion was caused by improperly placed charges or insufficient stemming {short fuse} that ignited coal dust. The blast shot through the mine, entering the entryway and adjoining rooms, exploding four {some sources state five} kegs of powder used by other miners. Initial reports stated that 96 men died in the accident; however, the confirmed fatality count was 40 men. Among the fatalities were six teenagers, including two boys aged 13. By 1889, the Kansas Legislature passed a bill requiring the use of shot firers {miners who load and fire drill holes} in coal mines, limiting shots to only one per day after all miners have left the mine. To date, the Frontenac tragedy remains the worst mining accident in Kansas history.

13. Geary Lake Falls is the largest man-made waterfall in Kansas. The waterfall, formed by the outlet of Geary State Fishing Lake {Geary County}, cascades approximately 35 feet {10.67 meters} into the water. The falls typically occur during the spring or after heavy rainfall.

14. The Quivira National Wildlife Refuge was established in 1955 and reached its present size of approximately 22,135 acres {8,957.72 hectares} in 1998. The refuge, located in Stafford and Rice counties, is divided into two parts by Rattlesnake Creek and two shallow lakes {Big Salt Marsh and Little Salt Marsh}. The Quivira National Wildlife Refuge includes approximately 13,000 acres {5,260.91 hectares} of dunes covered with prairie grasses. On January 29, 2008, Cheyenne Bottoms and the Quivira National Wildlife Refuge were jointly named one of the 8 Wonders of Kansas.

15. Kansas has over 120,000 lakes {both natural and man-made}, ponds, and rivers. While most of the water sources are private ponds, there are four natural lakes {Cheyenne Bottoms, Lake Inman, Lake View Lake, and the Quivira National Wildlife Refuge}, 30 man-made lakes managed by the United States Army Corps of Engineers, seven reservoirs managed by the Bureau of Reclamation, three reservoirs managed by the Kansas Department of Wildlife and Parks, and two reservoirs located on private property. Milford Lake, commonly referred to as Milford Reservoir {located northwest of Junction City, Geary County}, is the largest man-made lake in Kansas. The reservoir covers approximately 15,700 acres {6,353.57 hectares} with a maximum depth of approximately 65 feet {19.81 meters}. Lake Inman {McPherson County} is Kansas's largest natural lake. The lake is approximately 1.5 miles {2.41 kilometers} in circumference, with a maximum depth of approximately 20 feet {6.10 meters}.

16. Cheyenne Bottoms {Barton County} is a large wetland that occupies a natural land sink spanning approximately 41,000 acres {16,592.11 hectares}. The wetlands are a key stop on the Central Flyway {a bird migration route} and provide a habitat for several endangered species, including the whooping crane. The Cheyenne Bottoms Wildlife Area covers approximately 19,857 acres {8,035.84 hectares} of the Cheyenne Bottoms. The Nature Conservancy owns an adjacent area of approximately 7,300 acres {2,954.21 hectares}.

17. The Garden of Eden {Russell County} is an outdoor sculpture exhibit built between 1905 and 1927. The garden contains approximately 200 concrete sculptures, a twelve-room house, a concrete barn, a concrete pyramid, and a concrete spring. The house's logs feature limestone quarried from Wilson Lake. On April 28, 1977, the Garden of Eden was placed on the U.S. National Register of Historic Places. The exhibit is considered

the 8th Wonder of Kansas Art and is open to the public {for a fee}.

18. Mount Sunflower is Kansas's highest natural point. The summit {Wallace County} has an elevation of approximately 4,039 feet {1,231.09 meters} and a prominence of approximately 19 feet {5.79 meters}. Temple Knob is the most prominent mountain located in Kansas, with a summit elevation of approximately 1,650 feet {502.92 meters} and a prominence of approximately 213 feet {64.92 meters}. Kansas's lowest point is located in the Verdigris River, technically south of Coffeyville {Montgomery County}, where the river exits the state into Oklahoma, at an elevation of approximately 680 feet {207.26 meters}.

19. Approximately 15 miles {24.14 kilometers} northeast of Great Bend {Barton County} is the geographic center of Kansas.

20. On September 3, 1970, Coffeyville {Montgomery County} reported a piece of hail falling during a hailstorm that weighed 1.7 pounds {771.11 grams}. It was estimated to have hit the ground at a speed of 105 MPH {168.98 km/h}.

RONDA SEXTON

## What Was Kansas Thinking

## Ten Crazy Laws In Kansas

1. All satellite antennae placed {installed} on any tract of land require a building permit from the City of Larned.

2. Paintball guns are outlawed in the city limits of Arkansas City.

3. The city of Wichita forbids any homeowner from having dead or broken trees on their property.

4. Overland Park city ordinance states, "Picketing a funeral is lawful as long as the picket occurs 61 minutes after the funeral has ended."

5. No child under the age of nine is permitted in a Shawnee City cemetery without being accompanied by a person 16 or older.

6. Wichita requires the Chief of Police to send restricted mail to anyone residing on a property deemed a "chronic nuisance property."

7. The city of Valley Center requires all potbellied pigs to have 10,000 square feet {929.03 square meters} of fenced open space per pig located about 500 feet {152.4 meters} from all residential dwellings.

8. Music generated from a car radio cannot be audible past a distance of 50 feet {15.24 meters} in Osage City.

9. The city of Coffeyville forbids anyone to "falsely represent themselves as a member of a fraternal organization."

10. Storing lumber in a private enclosure is illegal in Neodesha.


****Please note, these laws may no longer be on the books; however, they were a law during some point in Kansas history****

# Kentucky

RONDA SEXTON

*"Kentucky's natural beauty is a dance of rolling hills, lush forests, and winding rivers, where every sunset and every breeze feels like nature's gentle embrace."*

CHATGPT {AI Generator}

AMERICA THE BOLD, AMERICA THE BRAVE, AMERICA THE BEAUTIFUL

# Kentucky Stats

## Statehood:

Date Granted: June 1, 1792
Rank of Admission: Kentucky became the 15th state to join the United States

## State Capital:

Capital City: Frankfort {Franklin County}
Adopted date: June 20, 1792
Capitol Building Design Architect(s):
Frank Mills Andrews {Current Building}

## State Population:

Population: 4,505,836 {US Federal Census 2020}
Rank: 26th most populous in the United States

## Land Mass:

Total Land Mass: 40,411 square miles {104,664.01 square kilometers}
Rank: 37th in Rank of The Largest State(s) in the United States

AMERICA THE BOLD, AMERICA THE BRAVE, AMERICA THE BEAUTIFUL

## Lovely Weather of Kentucky

### Record Highest Temperature:

Date: July 28, 1930
Location: Greensburg {Green County}
Temperature: 114 degrees Fahrenheit {45.56 degrees Celsius}

### Record Lowest Temperature:

Date: January 19, 1994
Location: Shelbyville {Shelby County}
Temperature: -37 degrees Fahrenheit {-38.33 degrees Celsius}

### Record Snowfall:

Date: March 3, 1942
Location: Simers {Pike County}
Amount: 26.0 inches {66.04 centimeters} (within a 24-hour timeframe)

## Record Precipitation:

Date: March 1, 1997
Location: Louisville {Jefferson County}
Amount: 10.48 inches {26.62 centimeters} (within a 24-hour timeframe)

## Major Earthquake:

Date: July 27, 1980
Location: Bath County {1 mile or 1.609 Kilometers SW of Sharpsburg}
Magnitude: 5.0 {Richter Scale}

RONDA SEXTON

*Kentucky Pride*

### State Name Origin:

Kentucky derives from the Iroquois Native American word "Ken-tah-ten" meaning "Land of Tomorrow"

### State Nickname(S):

The Bluegrass State
The Tobacco State
The Hemp State

### State Slogan:

The Bluegrass State

### State Motto:

"Deo Gratiam Habeamus" {Let Us Be Grateful to God}
The unofficial State Motto is "United We Stand, Divided We Fall"

RONDA SEXTON

## Symbols of Kentucky

**State Bird:**

Northern Cardinal
"Cardinalis Cardinalis"
Adopted date: February 26, 1926

RONDA SEXTON

## State Flag:

Designed by: Jesse Cox Burgess
Adopted date: March 26, 1918

**State Flower:**

Goldenrod
"Solidago Gigantea"
Adopted date: May 16, 1926

**State Quarter:**

Release date: October 15, 2001
15th released quarter, honoring all 50 states
Themed: My Old Kentucky Home
Highlights: Stately Mansion, Federal Hill and a thoroughbred racehorse
Designed by: Various Kentucky citizens submitted designs for the state quarter. The top 12 designs were displayed in the front lobby of the Capitol and on the Internet, allowing citizens of Kentucky to cast votes for their favorite concepts.
Engraved by: T. James Ferrell

**State Song:**

My Old Kentucky Home
Written by: Stephen Collins Foster
Composed by: Stephen Collins Foster
Adopted date: March 19, 1928
Amended date: July 15, 1988

RONDA SEXTON

## State Tree:

Tulip Poplar
"Liriodendron tulipifera"
Adopted date: July 15, 1994

AMERICA THE BOLD, AMERICA THE BRAVE, AMERICA THE BEAUTIFUL

# *Kentucky Facts*

## Twenty Interesting Facts About Kentucky

1. The Kentucky Derby, inaugurated May 17, 1875, is the oldest continuously held horse race in the United States. Commonly nicknamed "The Fastest Two Minutes in Sports," the event is held at Churchill Downs {Louisville, Jefferson County} on the first Saturday in May.

2. At approximately 784 miles {1261.73 kilometers}, Kentucky Lake is the largest man-made lake in Kentucky. However, Lake Barkley is larger {by volume} by approximately 2,082,000 acre-foot {2.568 cubic kilometers}. Lake Cumberland has an estimated 1,255 miles {2,019.73 kilometers} of shoreline, which stretches across four counties {Clinton, Pulaski, Russell, and Wayne County}.

3. Mammoth Cave National Park {Edmonson, Hart, and Barren Counties} features the longest cave system {to date}. Mammoth Cave has approximately 365 miles {587.411 kilometers} of surveyed passageways and was declared a World Heritage site on October 27, 1981.

4. On May 14, 1988, a group of teenagers from North Hardin High School, James T. Alton Middle School, and Radcliff Middle School were on board the Assembly of God Church {Hardin County} bus. The teens were traveling with four adults from the church, heading to Kings Island Theme Park in Warren County, Ohio. The outbound trip was uneventful, with everyone spending the day at the theme park. By early evening, the group boarded the bus and began traveling home. At approximately 10:55 pm, an intoxicated driver, traveling in the wrong direction, collided with the church bus on Interstate 71 near Carrollton {Carroll County}. The crash caused the gasoline fuel tank on the church bus to be punctured, resulting in the

fuel supply igniting. The bus quickly caught on fire. Some passengers escaped through the central rear emergency door; however, many were unable to escape. In total, the crash killed 27 passengers {the intoxicated driver survived the wreck}. The wreck encouraged many residents to become active in the MADD {Mothers Against Drunk Driving} movement.

5. With an elevation of an estimated 4,145 feet {1,263.4 meters} above sea level and a prominence of approximately 1,905 feet {580.64 meters}, Black Mountain {Harlan County} is the highest natural point in the state of Kentucky. Kentucky's lowest elevation {approximately 257 feet or 78.33 meters}, is located in the Mississippi River at Kentucky Bend {Fulton County}.

6. Cumberland Falls {Harlan County} is Kentucky's largest waterfall. Located in the Daniel Boone National Forest, the waterfall measures approximately 68 feet {20.726 meters} tall with an estimated 125 feet {38.1 meters} in height during high water. During certain times, Cumberland Falls creates a natural phenomenon known as a moonbow. A moonbow, commonly known as a "moon rainbow" or "lunar rainbow", is a beam of light {created by the moon} most commonly seen two days before, on, or after a full moon.

7. According to the old Kentucky Transportation Cabinet road maps, the geographic center of Kentucky is located approximately 3 miles {4.83 kilometers} northwest of Lebanon {Marion County}; however, Campbellsville {Taylor County} disputes the claim and states Campbellsville is the actual geographic center of Kentucky.

8. Located in Covington {Kenton County} is the Roman Catholic St. Mary's Cathedral Basilica of the Assumption. The church is home to an estimated 67-foot {20.423 meters} by 24-foot {7.315 meters} handblown glass window featuring an image of The Ecumenical Council of Ephesus. The window was created by

Mayer and Company from Munich, Germany, and installed in 1911. and fully restored in 2001.

9. In 1849, a provision to the Kentucky constitution was made. According to the article {Kentucky and the Code Duello}, "The sort of people who felt the need to duel also tend to be those who ran for office." The anti-dueling oath {Kentucky Constitution Section 228} requires all officers of the state and all members of the bar to swear they have not fought a duel with deadly weapons within this state nor outside of it.

10. Located in Grant County, is a theme park featuring the Biblical Noah's Ark. The Ark Encounter is a large timber-frame structure featuring three decks and 132 bays. The replica is an estimated 510 feet {155.448 meters} in length, approximately 85 feet {25.908 meters} wide, and approximately 51 feet {15.545 meters} in height. On the first deck, visitors can see animal models {no live animals are located inside the ark}. The second deck features additional animal models, a replica of Noah's workshop, and a blacksmith. The third deck includes the Flood Geology exhibit featuring two fossils from the Wyoming Fossil Butte National Monument. The theme park was opened on July 7, 2016, and features the Ararat Ridge Zoo {petting zoo}, a zipline, and a virtual reality theater.

11. In the winter of 2009 {January 25-January 30}, 11 states in America were hit by an ice storm with Kentucky taking the majority of the blow. An estimated 500,000 residents lost power, causing several people to resort to using power generators or kerosene heaters inside their homes. As a result, many residents lost their lives to carbon monoxide poisoning. In total, Kentucky had 35 fatalities due to the ice storm.

12. Bluegrass, commonly known as "Kentucky Bluegrass," is not native to America. The Spanish Empire introduced seeds to mix with other grasses in the "New World". The grass produces

bluish-purple buds, which give off a blue cast among the fields.

13. On August 21, 1955, a family living in a farmhouse in Kelly {Christian County} was enjoying a night with a friend visiting from Pennsylvania. The friend decided to retrieve some water from the well outside as the family prepared to settle down for the evening. As he made his way to the well, he noticed a large shining object streak across the sky and appear to land in a small gully approximately .25 miles {.402 kilometers} from the farmhouse. The frightened man dropped his bucket and ran back to the house, informing the family what he just witnessed. The father {believing his friend was playing a joke} began laughing at the story. After several attempts to convince the family that he was not kidding. The friend gave up and told the family, "Okay, but I warn you". An estimated 15 minutes passed before the family dog began barking wildly {which was unusual for the dog}. The father jumped up and grabbed his shotgun before heading outside to investigate. The friend quickly followed, carrying his .22 target pistol. As the two men stepped on the front porch, they noticed an estimated 3-foot to 4-foot {.914 or 1.219 meter} creature walking toward them. They described the creature as having silver skin, large eyes, a long, thin mouth, long ears, hands like claws, and thin, short legs. The two men began firing upon the creature with no result. Next, they noticed approximately 10 to 12 creatures surrounding the home. The family decided on an escape plan, running for their vehicles, and driving to the local police station. The police decided to investigate the incident, where arriving to the home, they noticed the farmhouse was full of gunshot holes; however, they could not find any creatures. While investigating, the police reported hearing a series of gunshots and seeing strange lights in the sky. The police also noticed an odd luminous patch along the fence and a green glowing light in the woods; however, the origin of the light was never located. After three hours of investigating, the police left. Approximately 90 minutes later, the creatures returned and then disappeared at the break of

dawn. To date, the incident has never been solved.

14. Middlesboro {Bell County}, located in the Middlesboro Basin, is the only city in America built within a meteor crater. Middlesboro is located entirely between Pine Mountain and the Cumberland Mountains in the Middlesboro Basin {a meteorite crater}.

15. Approximately 12,000,000 acres {4,856,227.707 hectares}, or roughly 47 percent of Kentucky, is covered by forests. Blanton Forest {Harlan County} is considered the largest state nature preserve in Kentucky. Blanton Forest State Nature Preserve covers approximately 3,510 acres {1,420.447 hectares} and has an estimated 2,350 acres {951.011 hectares} of old-growth trees.

16. Man O' War was an American thoroughbred racehorse. The thoroughbred racehorse began his career on June 6, 1919, in a maiden race over five furlongs. Man o' War won his first race by six lengths, then three days later, entered the Keene Memorial Stakes, placing fourth place. Then, the thoroughbred racehorse won the Youthful States twelve days later and the Hudson States two days afterwards, winning 4 wins in 18 days. On August 13, 1919, Man O' War lost {by a half-length} to a horse adequately named "Upset". During the thouroughbred's racing career, Man O'War won 20 of 21 races, setting three world records, two US horse racing, and three track records. The horse was the unofficial 1920 American Horse of the Year and was honored as the Outstanding Athlete of the Year by the newspaper New York Times.

17. Kentucky Bend is an exclave {a territory that is separated from the majority portion of the territory and surrounded by the territory of another state or entity} located in Fulton County and is encircled by Tennessee and Missouri. The exclave is referred to by several names {New Madrid Bend, Bessie Bend, Madrid Bend, or Bubbleland} and is the extreme southwestern

corner of Kentucky. The Kentucky Bend covers an estimated 26.9 square miles {69.671 square kilometers}, and according to the US Federal Census 2020, has a population of 9 residents.

18. Fort Knox {Hardin, Meade, and Bullitt Counties} is commonly known as the Home of the United States Bullion Depository or the Gold Vault. Fort Knox was named in honor of the American Revolutionary War Chief of Artillery, who later became the first United States Secretary of War. In 1936, a depository was built by the US Treasury, and in 1937, the first shipment of gold {under the security of the 7th Cavalry Brigade| was deposited in the depository. During WWII, after the Japanese attack on Pearl Harbor, the Declaration of Independence, the Constitution of the United States, and the Gettysburg Address were moved to Fort Knox for safekeeping. Today, the Army and Marine Corps servicemembers use the facility for military training services.

19. The World Peace Bell, formally named the Millennium Bell, was cast in Nantes {France} on December 11, 1998 {the 50th anniversary of the Universal Declaration of Human Rights}. The bell was first rung in Nantes on March 20, 1999, before traveling by sea to the US port of New Orleans {Orleans Parish} Louisiana and featured in the city's Fourth of July celebration. The World Peace Bell was then transported by barge up the Mississippi and Ohio Rivers, stopping in 14 cities along the route. On August 1, 1999, the bell arrived in Newport {Campbell County} Kentucky, where it is still located {to date}. On January 1, 2000, the bell rang at midnight {celebrating the New Year} with 12 strokes heard an estimated 25 miles {40.234 kilometers} away. The World Peace Bell weighs an estimated 66,000 pounds {29,937.096 kilograms} and is approximately 12 feet {3.658 meters} wide, featuring inscriptions of important events from the past 1,000 years.

20. In 1819, a digger from Virginia was drilling saltwater

in the Cumberland River {McCreary County}. Approximately 536 feet {163.373 meters} deep, the digger struck oil. The oil began flowing into the river, catching the river on fire. Annoyed, the digger left the spot. Ten years later, on March 11, 1929, the digger began digging for saltwater near Burkesville {Cumberland County}. While digging, his drill broke through a layer of limestone, hitting oil. The oil gushed out of the hole, causing the first Kentucky oil gusher. The gusher lasted an estimated four days, streaming approximately 15 feet {4.572 meters} high and burning approximately one mile {1.609 kilometers} on the Cumberland River.

AMERICA THE BOLD, AMERICA THE BRAVE, AMERICA THE BEAUTIFUL

# What Was Kentucky Thinking

## Ten Crazy Laws In Kentucky

1. Paducah requires all city employees and officers to conduct their private and public affairs in a manner that does not disgrace or disrepute the city government.

2. No person shall bathe in any water owned by {or leased to} the Commonwealth of Kentucky Department of Parks.

3. Flatwood law states, "A parent or guardian of a minor commits an offense by {knowingly or unknowingly} allowing a minor to be in public after curfew."

4. In Owensboro, a seller cannot use the word "free" with the intent of selling a product.

5. The city of Baldwin banned all use of reptiles in any religious ceremonies.

6. Pursuing squirrels, rabbits, or birds is unlawful in the City of Georgetown.

7. The state of Kentucky declared all import, transport, or possession of African buffalo, cheetah, elephants, and Gila monsters {bearded lizards} illegal in the state {unless authorized by the Department of Fish and Wildlife}.

8. Hopkins County banned all residents from placing bicycles, tricycles, or motor vehicle parts in solid waste containers provided by the county.

9. In the State of Kentucky, all marriage licenses are valid for thirty days {including the date it was issued}.

10. No female shall appear in public wearing a bathing suit if the female weighs less than 90 pounds {40.823 kilograms} nor exceeds 200 pounds {90.718 kilograms}.

****Please note, these laws may no longer be on the books; however, they were a law during some point in Kentucky's history****

# *Louisiana*

*"Louisiana: a soulful blend of moss-draped oaks, vibrant bayous, and sun-kissed wetlands, where the rhythms of the land and water weave a story as rich and deep as its heritage."*

CHATGPT {AI Generator}

RONDA SEXTON

# Louisiana Stats

## Statehood:

Date Granted: April 30, 1812
Rank of Admission: Louisiana was the 18th state to join the United States.

## State Capital:

Capital City: Baton Rouge {East Baton Rouge Parish}
Adopted date: November 4, 1930
Capitol Building Design Architect(s):
Leon W. Weiss {Current Building}
Felix Julius Dreyfous {Current Building}
Solis Seiferth {Current Building}

## State Population:

Population: 4,657,757 {US Federal Census 2020}
Rank: 25th most populous in the United States

## Land Mass:

Total Land Mass: 47,717 square miles {123,586.463 square kilometers}
Rank: 31st in Rank of Largest State(s) in the United States

RONDA SEXTON

## Lovely Weather of Louisiana

### Record Highest Temperature:

Date: August 10, 1936
Location: Plain Dealing {Bossier Parish}
Temperature: 114 degrees Fahrenheit {45.56 degrees Celsius)

### Record Lowest Temperature:

Date: February 13, 1899
Location: Minden {Webster Parish}
Temperature: -16 degrees Fahrenheit {-26.67 degrees Celsius}

### Record Snowfall:

Date: February 2, 1895
Location: Houma {Terrebonne Parish}
Amount: 16.0 inches {40.64 centimeters} (within a 24-hour timeframe)

### Record Snowfall:

Date: February 14, 1895
Location: Shell Beach {Vermilion Parish}
Amount: 16.0 inches {40.64 centimeters} (within a 24-hour timeframe)

### Record Precipitation:

Date: August 28-29, 1962
Location: Hackberry {Cameron Parish}
Amount: 22.0 inches {55.88 centimeters} (within a 24-hour timeframe)

### Major Earthquake:

Date: October 19, 1930
Location: Assumption Parish {7 miles or 11.265 kilometers south of Donaldsonville, Ascension Parish}
Magnitude: 4.2 {Richter Scale}

AMERICA THE BOLD, AMERICA THE BRAVE, AMERICA THE BEAUTIFUL

*Louisiana Pride*

### State Name Origin:

Louisiana is named in honor of King Louis XIV {King of France 1643-1715}

### State Nickname(S):

The Pelican State
The Bayou State
The Creole State

### State Slogan:

The Pelican State

### State Motto:

Union, Justice, and Confidence

AMERICA THE BOLD, AMERICA THE BRAVE, AMERICA THE BEAUTIFUL

# Symbols of Louisiana

RONDA SEXTON

## State Bird:

Brown Pelican
"Pelecanus occidentalis"
Adopted date: July 27, 1966

## State Flag:

Designed by: Replica of the State Seal
Adopted date: November 22, 2010

RONDA SEXTON

**State Flower:**

Southern Magnolia
"Magnolia grandiflora"
Adopted date: July 12, 1900

**State Quarter:**

Release date: May 30, 2002
18th released quarter, honoring all 50 states
Themed: Louisiana Purchase
Highlights: Brown Pelican, a trumpet, and the outline of the Louisiana Purchase
Designed by: John Mercanti
Engraved by: John Mercanti

## State Song:

Give Me Louisiana
Written by: Doralice Fontane
Composed by: John Croom
Adopted date: July 9, 1970

**State Song:**

You are My Sunshine
Written by: Jimmy H. Davis and Charles Mitchell
Composed by: Charles Mitchell
Adopted date: July 14, 1977

RONDA SEXTON

## State Tree:

Bald Cypress
"Taxodium distichum"
Adopted date: May 26, 1963

AMERICA THE BOLD, AMERICA THE BRAVE, AMERICA THE BEAUTIFUL

# Louisiana Facts

## Twenty Interesting Facts About Louisiana

1. The Louisiana State Capitol Building, standing at an estimated 450 feet {137.16 meters} tall, featuring 34 stories, currently holds the record as the tallest state capital in the United States. The building was inaugurated on May 16, 1932, and cost an estimated $5 million {1932 USD} to construct. On June 9, 1978, the Louisiana State Capitol Building and Gardens {official name} was added to the US National Register of Historic Places.

2. Louisiana does not use counties as their local governments but instead uses political subdivisions termed "Parishes". On March 31, 1807, the territory featured 19 parishes. On April 30, 1812, Louisiana was admitted to the Union with 25 parishes. In 1816, the first official map featuring the term parish was published. Then, in 1912, the last three parishes {Allen, Beauregard, and Jefferson} were formed, bringing the total number of parishes to 64.

3. On August 29, 2005, Hurricane Katrina breached 53 different flood protection structures around New Orleans {Orleans Parish}, submerging an estimated 80% of the city. The hurricane caused an estimated $100 billion in damages and eroded approximately 73 square miles {189.069 square kilometers} of Louisiana coastland. Louisiana's reported total death toll is undetermined; however, it is estimated between 986 and 1,577 deaths in the state, with several hundred residents remaining unknown or missing.

4. Louisiana has 15 lakes located within the state. Lake Pontchartrain is the largest lake with an estimated maximum length of 40 miles {64.374 kilometers} and a maximum width of approximately 24 miles {38.624 kilometers}. The lake covers a surface area of an estimated 630 square miles {1,631.693 square

meters} and features an estimated maximum depth of 65 feet {19.812 meters}.

5. Louisiana has been governed under 11 different flags since 1541. Flag of Castile and Leon {1492-1541}, White Fleur de Lis {1672-1762}, Spanish Flag {1763-1803}, British Flag {1763-1779}, French tricolor {November 30, 1803 – December 20, 1803}, United States Flag {representing 15 stars and 15 stripes} {1803-1861}, Flag of West Florida aka Bonnie Blue {September 1810-December 1810}, National Flag of Louisiana {1861}, Confederate States of America {1863- 1865}, the Louisiana Flag {1912 to present}, and the current United States Flag {1861 to present}.

6. On January 22, 1812, the first Louisiana constitution was signed by Louisiana delegates. The sitting US President transmitted the proceedings and constitution to Congress on March 4, 1812. Since 1812, nine more constitutions have been written {amended, changed, and adopted}. The current version of the Louisiana Constitution was ratified on April 20, 1974, and placed into effect on January 1, 1975. To date, Louisiana has adopted more written constitutions than any other state.

7. The geographic center of Louisiana is located approximately 3 miles {4.83 kilometers} south-east of Marksville {Avoyelles Parish}.

8. Louisiana's highest natural summit is Driskill Mountain, located in Bienville Parish. The natural summit features an elevation of approximately 535 feet {163.07 meters} and an estimated prominence of 225 feet 68.58 meters. New Orleans {Orleans Parish} has the lowest elevation in Louisiana. According to different studies, the lowest elevation is estimated to be approximately 1 foot {.305 meters} and 7 feet {2.133 meters} below sea level.

9. According to local legend, during the 1700s a group of albino dwarves moved to East New Orleans {Orleans Parish}. Over the years, the dwarves interbred among themselves until their offspring no longer resembled humans in appearance. A group of East New Orleans residents were scared of the dwarves, stating the dwarves had been created by the devil himself. The residents began protesting to the city council to abolish the dwarves to a secluded area in the woods. The city council complied with their wishes and banished the dwarves to a small area in the woods. Over the years, the city continued to grow, making the wooded area to grow smaller. A road {Grunch Road} was erected through the woods connecting several sections of the city, passing next to the dwarf village. As time went on, Grunch Road became a popular teenage hangout, where children gathered and hung out with other peers. Soon, people began to go missing, and the teenagers started reporting seeing a deformed creature in the woods. The creature was described as having the average height of a human with solid white skin, red eyes, no nose, and an abnormally large mouth. Some describe the creature as goat-like with leathery or scaly black-gray skin and sharp spines, long horns, and quills running down its back. Others reported the beast looked like a monkey with long fur, a tail, and bat-like wings. To date, people still claim to see deformed albinos, ghosts, and floating lights while parked on Grunch Road. Many also claim to hear strange cries and howls in the night skies along the roadway.

10. Louisiana does not have an official language. Three other languages besides English are commonly spoken in the state: {French, Spanish, and Vietnamese}.

11. An estimated two million alligators reside in Louisiana. Gator Country {Caddo and Bossier Parish} proclaim to be the largest alligator park in Louisiana. The park houses approximately 250 American alligators, lizards, snakes, tortoises, and goats {to date}. The estimated 7-acre {2.833

hectares} farm allows visitors to feed the alligators several times throughout the day and wade in water with baby gators.

12. The United States judicial system is primarily based on the Common Law System {a British style of judicial governing} and used in all US states, except Louisiana. The state features a "a hybrid judicial governing" that is influenced by the Napoleonic Code and the Common Law system.

13. In 1682, France claimed the Louisiana Terrority along with some of the land to the east. Then, in 1762, France ceded the land to Spain during the Seven Years War. On October 1, 1800, the leaders of France and Spain signed the Treaty of San Ildefonso, transferring the land back to France. On May 2, 1803, the United States purchased the land from France. The purchase, commonly known as the Louisiana Purchase, cost $15 million, or an estimated three cents per acre {approximately 828,000 square miles or 2,589,988.11 square kilometers}. Under the purchase, 15 states {some in full, others partial} were formed: {Arkansas, Colorado, Iowa, Missouri, Kansas, Louisiana, Minnesota, Montana, Nebraska, New Mexico, North Dakota, Oklahoma, Texas, South Dakota, and Wyoming}.

14. Traditionally in Christian cemeteries, tombstones face east to west. According to legend, the position of the graves is a pagan ritual, so the departed would face the rising sun; however, others claim it was due to the Biblical claim that the second coming of Christ would be from the east. The Saint Joseph's Cemetery {Rayne, Acadia Parish} features crypts facing north to south. There are many theories as to why the crypts were placed wrong. Some say the grave diggers misunderstood the instructions and made a 90-degree mistake. Others claim in 1880, as the railroad bypassed the town, the cemetery was moved and the crypts were misplaced. According to Ripley's Believe it or Not, St. Joseph's Cemetery is the only Christian cemetery in the United States facing the wrong way.

15. Kisatchie National Forest {Grant, Natchitoches, Winn, Rapides, Vernon, Claiborne, and Webster Parishes} is Louisiana's only national forest. Established June 10, 1930, the forest covers approximately 604,000 acres {244,430.128 hectares} and has five ranger districts {Calcasieu, Caney, Catahoula, Kisatchie, and Winn}.

16. On November 21, 1980, a Texaco oil rig accidentally caused a sinkhole to form in Lake Peigneur {Iberia Parish}. The drill on the rig became jammed, causing a series of popping noises followed by the tilting of the platform. As the oil rig began to submerge into the lake, it penetrated a main shaft of the Diamond Crystal salt mine, expanding an estimated 14-inch {35.56 centimeters} hole in the salt dome. As the lake water began rushing into the mine, 50 miners quickly escaped using mine carts and an elevator. In the end, the crew turned an estimated 10-foot {3.048 meters} deep freshwater lake into approximately 200-foot {60.96 meters} deep saltwater lake. Texaco agreed to pay $45 million to the mine owners and other local businesses.

17. The Mississippi River's traditional source begins in Lake Itasca {northern Minnesota} flowing into the Gulf of Mexico, approximately 100 miles {160.93 kilometers} from New Orleans {Orleans Parish}. The river flows through the entire eastern side of Louisiana.

18. Isle de Jean Charles {Terrebonne Parish} has lost approximately 98% of its landmass {about the size of Manhattan overall} due to saltwater intrusion and rising sea levels.

19. On March 2, 1699, a celebration in honor of Fat Tuesday {Mardi Gras} was held in Plaquemines Parish. In 1703, the first documented Mardi Gras festival was recorded in Mobile, {Mobile County} Alabama. By the 1730's the town of New

Orleans {Orleans Parish} began celebrating a Mardi Gras festival. The carnival-style celebration, consists of multiple large parades, masquerade balls, and the tradition of throwing beads, doubloons, plastic cups, moon pies, and small toys to the crowd. The city continues to host the celebration each year, with thousands of visitors from around the world attending.

20. The Atchafalaya Basin {south central Louisiana} is a wetland and river delta area where the Atchafalaya River and the Gulf of Mexico converge. The basin contains approximately 70% forest and 30% marsh along with open water. {the basin is a continually growing delta system, so forestry and marshlands continue to change}. Atchafalaya Basin is the United States' largest river swampland containing the largest contiguous bottomland hardland forest in North America.

RONDA SEXTON

# What was Louisiana Thinking

## Ten Crazy Laws In Louisiana

1. Stealing an alligator can result in 10 years in jail.

2. In the city of Zachary, anyone who is the aggressor in a fight cannot claim the fight was in self-defense.

3. It is unlawful for a person under the age of 16 to enter a bowling alley in Amite City.

4. In New Orleans, all bears, wolverines, badgers, lions, and tigers are illegal to own.

5. The right of the people to preserve, foster, and promote their respective historic languages is recognized by the Louisiana Constitution.

6. Raising, keeping, or maintaining hogs or swine is considered a nuisance in the city of Addis.

7. Bomb bags are prohibited from being thrown from floats during Mardi Gras parades.

8. In Lafayette, walking, driving, or entering upon railroad tracks is illegal.

9. In Assumption Parish, an employer who houses five or more non-speaking English employees must provide 24-hour access to an interpreter.

10. Caddo Parish bans wearing all saggy clothing in public.


****Please note, these laws may no longer be on the books; however, they were a law during some point in Louisiana's history****

# Maine

*"Maine's beauty is a masterpiece of rugged coastlines, towering pines, and tranquil waters, where every breeze carries the wild, untamed spirit of the sea."*

CHATGPT {AI Generator}

AMERICA THE BOLD, AMERICA THE BRAVE, AMERICA THE BEAUTIFUL

# Maine Stats

## Statehood:

Date Granted: March 15, 1820
Rank of Admission: Maine became the 23rd state to join the United States.

## State Capital:

Capital City: Augusta {Kennebec County}
Adopted date: February 24, 1827
Capitol Building Design Architect(s):
Charles Bulfinch {Current Building}

## State Population:

Population: 1,362,359 {US Federal Census 2020}
Rank: 42nd most populous in the United States

## Land Mass:

Total Land Mass: 35,128 square miles {90,981.102 square kilometers}
Rank: 39th in Rank of The Largest State(s) in the United States

AMERICA THE BOLD, AMERICA THE BRAVE, AMERICA THE BEAUTIFUL

## Lovely Weather of Maine

## Record Highest Temperature:

Date: July 4, 1911
Location: North Bridgton {Cumberland County}
Temperature: 105 degrees Fahrenheit {40.56 degrees Celsius}

## Record Highest Temperature:

Date: July 10, 1911
Location: North Bridgton {Cumberland County}
Temperature: 105 degrees Fahrenheit {40.56 degrees Celsius}

## Record Lowest Temperature:

Date: January 16, 2009
Location: Big Black River {Aroostoock County}
Temperature: -50 degrees Fahrenheit {-45.56 degrees Celsius}

### Record Snowfall:

Date: December 22, 2008
Location: Eustis {Franklin County}
Amount: 41.8 inches {106.172 centimeters} (within a 24-hour timeframe)

### Record Precipitation:

Date: October 20-21, 1996
Location: Portland {Cumberland County}
Amount: 13.32 inches {33.832 centimeters} (within a 24-hour timeframe)

### Major Earthquake:

Date: December 12, 1947
Location: Piscataquis County {3 miles or 4.828 Kilometers NE of Sangerville}
Magnitude: 4.5 {Richter Scale}

RONDA SEXTON

*Maine Pride*

### State Name Origin:

Maine is named in honor of the French province "Maine"

### State Nickname(S):

The Pine Tree State
The Border State
Old Dirigo State

### State Slogan:

The Pine Tree State

### State Motto:

"Dirigo" {I Lead or I Direct}

RONDA SEXTON

# Symbols of Maine

**State Bird:**

Black-Capped Chickadee
"Parus Atricapillus"
Adopted date: April 6, 1927

RONDA SEXTON

## State Flag:

Designed by: Replica of the State Coat of Arms
Adopted date: June 16, 1909

**State Flower:**

White Pine Cone and Tassel
"Pinus Strobus, Linnaeus"
Adopted date: February 1, 1895

**State Quarter:**

Released date: June 2, 2003
23rd released quarter, honoring all 50 states
Themed: "Pemaquid Point Light"
Highlight: Pemaquid Point Light atop a granite coast, and a schooner at sea
Designed by: Daniel Carr
Engraved by: Donna Weaver

**State Song:**

State of Maine
Written by: Roger Vinton Snow
Composed by: Roger Vinton Snow
Adopted date: April 5, 1937

RONDA SEXTON

## State Tree:

Eastern White Pine
"Pinaceae Pinus Strobus"
Adopted date: July 21, 1945

## Maine Facts

## Twenty Interesting Facts About Maine

1. According to Yankee Magazine, an article was published in January 1972, stating the first place to see the sunrise in Maine depends on the time of year. Between October 7 and March 6, the best place is the Cadillac Mountain {Acadia National Park}; between March 7 and March 24, head to the West Quoddy Head Lighthouse {Washington County}. Between March 25 and September 18, you should travel to Mars Hill {Aroostook County}. Then, between September 19 and October 6, you should return to the West Quoddy Head Lighthouse.

2. On the southwestern border of Maine lies New Hampshire. New Hampshire is the only American state that shares a border with Maine. The Canadian province of New Brunswick lies north of Maine, and the Canadian province of Quebec is northwest of the state. The Atlantic Ocean lies on the southeastern border of Maine. Maine's tidal coastline {along the Atlantic Ocean} spans approximately 3,478 miles {5,597.3 kilometers}, including an estimated 230 miles {370.15 kilometers} of ocean coastline. Maine is the northeasternmost state in the contiguous United States and the largest state in the New England area.

3. In the Fall of 1954, Maine was struck back to back with two Category 2 hurricanes. On September 1, 1954, Hurricane Carol struck the state of Maine, killing one person and causing $10 million in damages {1954 USD}. Ten days later, on September 11, 1954, Hurricane Edna struck Eastport {Washington County}, killing eight people and causing $15 million in damages {1954 USD}.

4. Aroostook County {approximately 6,828 square miles or 17,684.44 square kilometers} is larger than Connecticut and Rhode Island {combined total of approximately 6,757 square

miles or 17,500.55 square kilometers}.

5. Maine has approximately 1,882 mountains within the state borders. Mount Katahdin {Piscataquis County} is Maine's tallest mountain. The mountain peak has an elevation of an estimated 5,267 feet {1,605.382 meters} with a prominence of approximately 4,288 feet (1,306.98 meters). Mount Agamenticus {York County} features an elevation of an estimated 692 feet {210.922 meters} and an estimated prominence of 515 feet {156.972 meters}. The mountain summit is the lowest mountain peak in Maine.

6. Lafayette National Park was established on February 26, 1919. On January 19, 1929, the park was renamed the Acadia National Park. Acadia National Park is the only registered national park located in Maine. Although the Appalachian National Scenic Trail, Katahdin Woods and Waters National Monument, and Saint Croix Island International Historic Site are sometimes referred to as National Parks, they are not designated as such. The park consists of approximately 49,075 acres {19.859.948 hectares}, or approximately 76.7 square miles {198.652 square kilometers}. An estimated 861.46 acres {348.620 hectares} are privately owned {2017}. Acadia National Park features Cadillac Mountain {the tallest mountain on the Atlantic Coast}, and Mount Desert Island {the largest island off the coast of Maine}. The Acadia National Park is known for hiking, bicycling, horseback riding on carriage roads, rock climbing, fishing, canoeing, sea kayaking, and guided boat tours. In 2020, an estimated 2,669,034 visitors visited the National Park.

7. Maine is the easternmost state of the United States. Quoddy Head {Washington County} is the most easterly point in the United States. Quoddy Head is approximately 3,154 miles {5,075.87 kilometers} from El Beddouza {Africa} and approximately 3,406 miles {5,481.43 kilometers} from Morocco {North Africa}. It is closer to Africa than any other area

in the United States. Key West {Monroe County} Florida is approximately 4,358 miles {7,013.521 kilometers} from El Beddouza {Africa} and approximately 4,491 miles {7,227.564 kilometers} from Morocco {North Africa}.

8. As of 2020, there are 32 state parks, 10 National Wildlife Refuges, 1 National Forest, 4 National Parks, and 3,166 coastal islands {according to the Maine Coastal Island Registry} located in Maine. Baxter State Park {Piscataquis County} is the state's largest state park. The state park covers an estimated 209,501 acres {84,782.047 hectares} and was established on March 3, 1931. Moosehorn National Wildlife Refuge is Maine's largest wildlife refuge. The wildlife refuge {Washington County} covers an estimated 28,751 acres {11,635.117 hectares} and was created in 1937. White Mountain National Forest is located in three counties in New Hampshire {Grafton, Coos, and Carroll counties} and one county in Maine {Oxford County}. The National Forest is the only national forest located in both states. Acadia National Park is the only national park located in Maine. Acadia National Park {Hancock and Knox Counties} was established on January 19, 1929, and covers an estimated 49,075 acres {19,859.948 hectares}. Mount Desert Island {Hancock County} is the largest island off the coast of Maine. The island covers an estimated 108 square miles {279.719 square kilometers}. Mount Desert Island is the 52nd-largest island in the United States.

9. The worst natural disaster {to date} in Maine's history happened between January 4 and January 10, 1998, and is commonly referred to as The Ice Storm of 1998. During the storm, some areas reported up to 80 hours of continuous freezing rain, ice, and snow. The storm knocked out electricity to over 700,000 Maine residents, resulting in no running water and little {to no} heat. In total, the storm caused $5-7 billion {2005 USD} in damages, 28 deaths in Canada, and 18 deaths in the United States.

10. In 1808, a lighthouse was constructed in Washington County to help guide ships through the Quoddy Narrows {an irregular channel between West Quoddy Head and Liberty Point (Campobello Island)}. The West Quoddy Head Light was replaced in 1858 by a second lighthouse, which is still being used today. The lighthouse was painted red with white stripes, and commonly known as the "Candy Cane" Lighthouse. On July 4, 1980, the Candy Cane lighthouse was added to the National Register of Historic Places.

11. Located in Piscataquis County {approximately 18 miles or 28.968 kilometers north of Dover-Foxcroft} is the geographical center of Maine.

12. Saint Croix Island International Historic Site {Washington County}, commonly known as Dochet Island, is a small uninhabited island near the mouth of the Saint Croix River. The river forms part of the Canada-United States border, separating Maine from New Brunswick {Canada}. The island is approximately 6.5 acres {2.630 hectares} and has no public access.

13. Maine has an estimated 2,500 lakes and approximately 5,000 rivers and streams. Moosehead Lake {Piscataquis County} is Maine's largest natural lake. The lake covers an estimated 75,451 acres {30,533.936 hectares}, featuring an estimated maximum depth of 246 feet {74.98 meters}, an estimated maximum length of 40 miles {64.374 kilometers}, and an estimated maximum width of 10 miles {16.09 kilometers}.

14. Maine is the only state in the United States whose name has one syllable. It also ties with Texas, and Idaho in second place with the fewest letters in its name {Ohio, Utah, and Iowa tie for first place}.

15. According to local legend, a group of fairies haunts the woods of Maine. The fairies are known to be good-hearted but tend to be a bit mischievous at times. Legend states when you encounter a mischievous fairy, you should leave small gifts {like fairy cakes or fairy houses} in the woods for them.

16. After 108 days of no reasonable rainfall, several small fires began in Maine. On October 23, 1947, hurricane-force winds caused the fires to span through central and southern areas of Maine. Finally, on October 29, 1947, rain began to fall, causing the fires to be extinguished. In total, approximately 200,000 acres {80.937.128 hectares} were burned {primarily in York County}, over 2,500 residents lost their homes, and an estimated $11 million {1947 USD} in damages occurred. The tragic event, commonly known as "The Year Maine Burned" is Maine's largest forest fire disaster {to date}.

17. Machias Seal Island is in disputed waters by the United States and Canada. Located approximately 10 miles {16.09 kilometers} from Cutler {Washington County} and an estimated 12 miles {19.312 kilometers} from the Grand Manan Island {New Brunswick, Canada}, both countries claim the island. Even though all residents have the right to dual citizenship, the island are unhabitable except for the lighthouse keepers {two Canadian Coast Guards}.

18. Maine's tallest waterfall is Katahdin Falls {Piscataquis County} with an estimated 800 foot {243.84 meters} vertical drop. Followed by Moxie Falls {Somerset County} and Angel Falls {Franklin County}, both tied with a vertical drop of approximately 90 feet {27.43 meters}.

19. Opened on November 16, 1931, the Waldo-Hancock Bridge was the first long-span suspension bridge erected in Maine. The bridge spans a length of an estimated 2,040 feet {621.79 meters} with a width of approximately 20 feet {6.1 meters},

connecting Verona Island {Hancock County} to Prospect {Waldo County}. The original toll ranged from 10 cents for a horse vehicle {including driver} to 50 cents for an auto vehicle or tractor {estimated 26,000 pounds or 11,793.4 kilograms}. In 2002, state official believed the bridge was beyond rehabilitation and needed to be closed. On December 30, 2006, a new bridge was opened to traffic, causing the Waldo-Hancock Bridge to be permanently closed. On February 12, 2012, the Maine Department of Transportation announced the demolition of the bridge. Then in June 2013, the Waldo-Hancock Bridge's flag poles were removed, finishing the demolition process.

20. Old Sow is the largest tidal whirlpool in the Western Hemisphere. The whirlpool is located off the southwestern shore of Deer Island, New Brunswick, {Canada}, and the northeastern shoreline of Moose Island {Washington County}, Maine. Old Sow occurs where the water exchanges between Passamaquoddy Bay and the Bay of Fundy, forming a tidal whirlpool with a diameter of approximately 250 feet {76.2 meters}. Old Sow is one of five significant tidal whirlpools located in the world.

RONDA SEXTON

# What was Maine Thinking

## Ten Crazy Laws Of Maine

1. Marking or removing any building structure, table, bench, or sign in a public park is banned in the city of Auburn.

2. The town of Freeport banned all food vendors from serving or selling prepared food in Styrofoam containers.

3. Old Orchard Beach requires the regulation of newspaper vending machines for the safety and welfare of pedestrians.

4. Noisy dogs for an excess of ten minutes are considered a public nuisance in the town of Eliot unless it is in the presence of someone trespassing or threatening to trespass on private property.

5. All Native Americans are required to be electors in all county, state, and national elections.

6. It is unlawful for uninvited telephone or door-to-door solicitations for crematory or cemetery services.

7. The constitution of Maine gives all citizens the right to natural, inherent, and unalienable food.

8. Waterboro bans all "fighting words" within city parks and recreational spaces.

9. In the town of Orono, no two roads shall be named the same or have similar-sounding names.

10. The town of Brunswick has a cable television clause in the city ordinance, requiring cable franchisees to operate 24 hours a day, 7 days a week.

****Please note, these laws may no longer be on the books; however, they were a law during some point in Maine's history****

# Maryland

RONDA SEXTON

*"Maryland's beauty is found in the gentle embrace of its Chesapeake shores, the vibrant colors of autumn leaves, and the peaceful whisper of its mountains—a timeless reminder that nature's most perfect moments are often just around the corner."*

*CHATGPT {AI Generator}*

AMERICA THE BOLD, AMERICA THE BRAVE, AMERICA THE BEAUTIFUL

# Maryland Stats

## Statehood:

Granted date: April 28, 1788
Rank of Admission: Maryland became the 7th state to join the United States

## State Capital:

Capital City: Annapolis {Anne Arundel County}
Adopted date: November 23, 1783
Capital Building Design Architect(s):
Joseph Horatio Anderson {Current Building}

## State Population:

Population: 6,177,224 {US Federal Census 2020}
Ranked: 18th most populous in the United States

## Land Mass:

Total Land Mass: 10,455 square miles {27,078.326 square kilometers}

Ranked: 42nd in the United States of America

AMERICA THE BOLD, AMERICA THE BRAVE, AMERICA THE BEAUTIFUL

## Lovely Weather of Maryland

## Record Highest Temperature:

Record Highest Temperature:
Date: July 3, 1898
Location: Boettcherville {Frederick County}
Temperature: 109 degree Fahrenheit {42.78 degree Celsi

## Record Highest Temperature:

Date: August 6, 1918
Location: Keedysville {Washington County}
Temperature: 109 degrees Fahrenheit {42.78 degrees Celsius}

## Record Highest Temperature:

Date: August 6, 1918
Location: Cumberland {Allegany County}
Temperature: 109 degrees Fahrenheit {42.78 degrees Celsius}

## Record Highest Temperature:

Date: August 7, 1918
Location: Cumberland {Allegany County}
Temperature: 109 degrees Fahrenheit {42.78 degrees Celsius}

## Record Highest Temperature:

Date: July 10, 1936
Location: Frederick {Frederick County}
Temperature: 109 degrees Fahrenheit {42.78 degrees Celsius}

## Record Highest Temperature:

Date: July 10, 1936
Location: Cumberland {Allegany County}
Temperature: 109 degrees Fahrenheit {42.78 degrees Celsius}

## Record Lowest Temperature:

Date: January 13, 1912
Location: Oakland {Garrett County}
Temperature: -40 degrees Fahrenheit {-40 degrees Celsius}

## Record Snowfall:

Date: March 29, 1942
Location: Clear Spring {Washington County}
Amount: 31 inches {78.74 centimeters} (within a 24-hour time frame)

## Record Precipitation:

Date: July 26-27, 1897
Location: Jewell {near Friendship, Anne Arundel County}
Amount: 14.75 inches {37.465 centimeters} (within a 24-hour time frame)

## Major Earthquake:

Date: July 16, 2010
Location: Montgomery County {3 miles or 4.828 kilometers NNW of Barnesville}
Magnitude: 3. 4 {Richter Scale}

AMERICA THE BOLD, AMERICA THE BRAVE, AMERICA THE BEAUTIFUL

## Maryland Pride

### State Name Origin:

Maryland is named, in honor of Queen Henrietta Maria {wife of King Charles I}

### State Nickname(S):

The Old Line State
The Free State
The Queen State

### State Slogan:

The Old Line State

### State Motto:

"Fatti Maschii, Parole Femine" {Strong Deeds, Gentle Words}

AMERICA THE BOLD, AMERICA THE BRAVE, AMERICA THE BEAUTIFUL

# Symbols of Maryland

RONDA SEXTON

## State Bird:

Baltimore Oriole
"Icterus galbula"
Adopted date: February 26, 1947

## State Flag:

Designed by George Calvert
Adopted date: November 25, 1904

RONDA SEXTON

## State Flower:

Black-Eyed Susan
"Rudbeckia hirta"
Adopted date: April 18, 1918

**State Quarter:**

Released date: March 13, 2000
7th quarter released, honoring all 50 states
Themed: The Old Line State
Higlights: Maryland Statehouse
Designed by: William J. Krawczewicz
Engraved by: Thomas D Rodgers

RONDA SEXTON

**State Song:**

Maryland, My Maryland
Written by: James Ryder Randall
Composed by: Melchior Franck
Adopted date: April 29, 1939
Repealed date: July 1, 2021

**State Tree:**

White Oak
"Quercus alba"
Adopted date: May 2, 1941

RONDA SEXTON

## Maryland Facts

## Twenty Interesting Facts About Maryland

1. According to Maryland's Geological Survey, the state has approximately 53 known caves, with the majority located primarily in the western part of Maryland {Allegany, Garrett, Frederick, and Washington Counties}. The largest cave in Maryland is Crabtree Cave, which features an estimated 4,200 feet {1,280.16 meters} of mapped passageways. The cave is protected by the state, and all visitors must obtain permission to enter. The only cave available for tourism is Crystal Grottoes Caverns {Washington County}, which opened to the public on April 2, 1922, offering several rooms to explore. Crystal Grottoes Caverns features the Blanket Room measuring an estimated 30 feet {9.144 meters} long and approximately 20 feet {6.096 meters} wide and is the largest area located in the cavern.

2. An estimated 53 general state parks, covering approximately 97,784 acres {39,571.781 hectares}, are located in Maryland. Gunpowder Falls State Park {Baltimore and Harford Counties}, covering approximately 14,949 acres {6,049.646 hectares}, is currently the largest state park. It features an estimated 120 miles {193.121 kilometers} of trails for hiking, biking, and horseback riding. The smallest state park is Casselman River Bridge State Park {Garrett County}, covering approximately 4 acres {1.619 hectares}. The park preserves the Casselman River Bridge, a historic stone arch used as a transportation structure over the Casselman River.

3. An estimated 100 lakes are located in Maryland; however, there are no natural lakes—only man-made lakes formed by damming rivers. The largest lake is Deep Creek Lake {Garrett County}, which covers approximately 4,500 acres {1,821.087 hectares} and has an estimated 69 miles {111.045 kilometers}

of shoreline. Maryland's largest body of water is the Chesapeake Bay, covering approximately 4,479 square miles {11,600.557 square kilometers}. The Chesapeake Bay {which borders Maryland, Delaware, New York, Pennsylvania, West Virginia, and Virginia} is the largest estuary in the United States. It splits Maryland in half between the Delmarva Peninsula {eastern border} from Cape Henry, and Cape Charles {southern border}.

4. Maryland has two state battlefields, covering an estimated 2,474 acres {1,001.192 hectares}. On September 12, 1814, the Maryland Militia fought the invading British forces from behind a fence in Baltimore {Baltimore County} during the War of 1812. The North Point State Battlefield, preserves the battleground of the conflict, covering an estimated 9 acres {3.642 hectares}. The battlefield state park was open to the public on July 10, 2015, featuring a visitor center containing War of 1812 exhibits. The South Mountain State Battlefield {Frederick and Washington Counties} covers an estimated 2,465 acres {997.550 hectares} and preserves the sites of Union victories at the Battle of South Mountain on September 14, 1862, and the Battle of Antietam on September 17, 1862.

5. The geographic center of Maryland lies in Prince George's County, approximately 3.3 miles {5.311 kilometers} north of Bowie.

6. The Maryland Toleration Act {also known as the Act Concerning Religion} was the first law in the United States requiring religious tolerance for Christians. The act was passed on April 21, 1649, by the Maryland colony in St. Mary's County. It allowed freedom of worship for all Christians but sentenced anyone who denied Jesus to death. The act was repealed in 1692 following the Glorious Revolution and the Protestant Revolution. On December 15, 1791, the United States government passed the First Amendment to the United States Constitution, which prevents the government from making

laws that establish religion or prohibit its free exercise.

7. Buckel's Bog in Garrett County was believed to have been a shallow glade {a clearing within a forest} or a periglacial lake {a lake bordering a glacier}. The bog covers an estimated 160 acres {64.750 hectares}, and is the remnant of the only known natural lake in Maryland.

8. On July 30, 2016, Ellicott City {Howard County} experienced a torrential thunderstorm. The storm's slow-moving pace caused the Patapsco River to rise an estimated 13 feet {3.962 meters}, prompting the National Weather Service to issue a flash flood emergency for the city. Ellicott City received approximately 6.5 inches {16.51 centimeters} of rain within a few hours, destroying the downtown area and killing two people.

9. In 1790, the United States federal government ceded land from Maryland to form the District of Columbia. Today, Montgomery County, Prince George's County, Frederick County, Charles County, and Calvert County, along with portions of Virginia, West Virginia, and Washington, D.C., are part of the Washington-Arlington-Alexandria, DC-VA-MD-WV metropolitan statistical area, commonly known as the National Capital Region.

10. Mount Airy is commonly referred to as the "four-county area" due to the mailing area consisting of portions of four different counties: Frederick, Carroll, Montgomery, and Howard.

11. According to legend, a scientist working at the Beltsville Agricultural Research Center fused the DNA of a goat with his own. The scientist mutated into what is commonly known as the Maryland Goatman {or Goatman of Maryland} and is said to roam the back roads of Beltsville {Prince George's County} carrying an ax. There are multiple stories of the Goatman. One story states in 1977, two couples parked on Fletchertown Road

reportedly heard scratching outside their car, and when the driver turned on the lights, they saw the Goatman. The Goatman started running toward them and struck the car with an ax. Another story describes the Goatman as an old hermit who lives in the woods, scaring away anyone who enters to close to his home.

12. Cunningham Falls State Park {Frederick County} is a state park covering an estimated 6,080 acres {2,460.489 hectares}. The park features Maryland's largest cascading waterfall, Cunningham Falls, commonly known as McAfee Falls, which has an elevation of approximately 78 feet {23.774 meters}. According to local legend, the waterfalls were named after a photographer who frequently photographed the falls.

13. Since 1950, Maryland has been struck by 142 hurricanes, tropical storms, and tropical depressions. Hurricane Agnes {June 2, 1972} was the deadliest of these storms, killing 19 people {some reports claim 21}. Hurricane Irene {August 28, 2011} was the most damaging, causing $151 million {2011 USD} in damages. Hurricane Hazel {October 15, 1954} had the strongest winds, reaching an estimated 75 MPH {120.701 km/h}.

14. Approximately 43% of Maryland's landmass {about 2.7 million acres or 1.099 million hectares} is covered by forests. However, 16 of Maryland's 23 counties border tidal waters, with the combined length of tidal shoreline, including islands, is estimated at 4,431 miles {7,131.003 kilometers}.

15. Potomac State Forest {Garrett County} is a state forest covering an estimated 11,535 acres {4,668.489 hectares}. The forest features the Crabtree Woods, the largest surviving remnant of old-growth forest in Maryland, covering an estimated 500 acres {202.343 hectares} of mixed Appalachian hardwoods, including sugar maple, red oak, basswood, and

cucumber tree.

16. Between February 7 and February 8, 1904, a fire broke out in Baltimore {Baltimore County}. The fire burned for approximately 30 hours, spanning 70 city blocks {approximately 140 acres or 56.656 hectares} and destroying 1,545 buildings. The damage cost exceeded $150 million {1904 USD}, equivalent to an estimated $4.362 billion {2020 USD}. The Great Baltimore Fire is considered one of Maryland's largest fires.

17. Hoye Crest {located on Backbone Mountain in Garrett County} is the highest natural elevation in Maryland. The mountain summit reaches an estimated 3,360 feet {1,024.128 meters} above sea level, with a prominence of approximately 80 feet {24.384 meters}.

18. Located approximately 10 miles {16.093 kilometers} west of Crisfield {Somerset County} is Smith Island, the only inhabited offshore island in Maryland. Access to the mainland is available by boat only.

19. Assateague Island is shared by both Maryland {to the north} and Virginia {to the south}. The barrier island's north entrance is approximately 8 miles {12.874 kilometers} south of Ocean City {Worcester County}, Maryland and the south entrance is approximately 2 miles {3.219 kilometers} east of Chincoteague {Accomack County}, Virginia.

20. Bloody Point Hole, located at the bottom of the Chesapeake Bay, is the lowest elevation in Maryland. It is a natural depression approximately 1 mile {1.609 kilometers} west-southwest of Kent Island {Queen Anne's County} and is approximately 174 feet {53.035 meters} below sea level.

RONDA SEXTON

# What was Maryland Thinking

## Ten Crazy Laws In Maryland

1. The town of Chevy Chase requires all residents to have a parking permit for their health, safety, and welfare.

2. Mount Rainer bans all residents from performing tree pruning.

3. The town of Woodsboro has declared dirt a nuisance and a danger to public health.

4. Recyclable solid waste, including cardboard, office paper, plants, and grass, cannot be collected by homeowners in Gaithersburg.

5. Baltimore County law states all sinks must maintain 65 degrees Fahrenheit {18.33 degrees Celsius} between the hours of 6:30 a.m. and 11:30 p.m.

6. The town of La Plata requires a community of three members for the city's Beautification Commission program; however, they are not paid for their services.

7. St. Mary's County requires all residents to remove all snow, ice, or other frozen precipitation from sidewalks within 72 hours after precipitation has ended.

8. Frostburg defines an unruly social gathering as "A party of 4 people causing an abnormal amount of foot or vehicle traffic."

9. Ocean City banned all ownership of snakes {exceeding 4 inches or 10.16 centimeters}, alligators, and crocodiles.

10. To construct any building in Prince George's County, the builder must provide evidence to the city council that the structure is rodent-proof.

****Please note, these laws may no longer be on the books; however, they were a law during some point in Maryland's history****

AMERICA THE BOLD, AMERICA THE BRAVE, AMERICA THE BEAUTIFUL

# Book II Resources

## Hawaii

Date of Statehood
Stienecker, D. L. (1996). First Facts about The States. United States: Scholastic
Rank of Admission
Stienecker, D. L. (1996). First Facts about The States. United States: Scholastic
State Capital
Aylesworth, T. G. (1990). State Capitals. United States: Gallery Books
State Capitol Building Architects
Goodsell, C. T. (2001). The American statehouse : interpreting democracy's temples. United Kingdom: University Press of Kansas
Population 2020
U.S Department of Commerce, United States Census Bureau (2020) Population and Housing State Data
Land Mass
U.S Department of Commerce, United States Census Bureau (2020) Population and Housing State
Highest Record Temperature
Burt, C. C., Stroud, M. (2004). Extreme Weather: A Guide & Record Book. United Kingdom: W.W. Norton.
Lowest Record Temperature
Burt, C. C., Stroud, M. (2004). Extreme Weather: A Guide & Record Book. United Kingdom: W.W. Norton.
Record Snowfall
National Oceanic and Atmospheric Adminstration, National Centers for Environmental Information {2020}: Snowfall Extremes
Record Precipitation
Cerveny, R. (2024). Judging Extreme Weather: Climate Science in Action. United Kingdom: Taylor & Francis.
Major Earthquake
Furumoto, A. S., Nielsen, N. N., Phillips, W. R. (1973). A Study of Past Earthquakes, Isoseismic Zones of Intensity, and Recommended Zones for Structural Design for Hawaii. United States: Hawaii Institute of Geophysics, University of Hawaii
State Name Origin
Shearer, B. F., Shearer, B. S. (2001). State Names, Seals, Flags, and Symbols: A Historical Guide. United States: ABC-CLIO
State Nicknames
Shearer, B. F., Shearer, B. S. (2001). State Names, Seals, Flags, and Symbols: A Historical Guide. United States: ABC-CLIO
State Slogan
Shearer, B. F., Shearer, B. S. (2001). State Names, Seals, Flags, and Symbols: A Historical Guide. United States: ABC-CLIO
State Motto
HAWAII STATE CHAPTER 5, EMBLEMS AND SYMBOLS, STATE MOTTO, SECTION 5-9
State Bird Research
Hawaii State Legislative; HRS_0005-0017. [§5-17] Statebird, L1988,c178,§1]
State Flag Illustration
"ST Abode Stock.com" Stock photos, royalty-free images,graphics,vectors,&videos; Retrieved Jun 17,2022

https://bit.ly/3h51Z7T
State Flag Research
Hawaii State CHAPTER 5, EMBLEMS AND SYMBOLS, STATE FLAG, SECTION § 3
State Flower Research
HAWAII STATE CHAPTER 5, EMBLEMS AND SYMBOLS, STATE FLOWER, SECTION §5-16 [L1988,c177,§1;amL2000,c165,§3]
State Quarter Illustration
"ST Abode Stock.com" Stock photos, royalty-free images,graphics,vectors,&videos; Retrieved Jun 21,2022
https://bit.ly/3iKOjz8
State Quarter Research
Noles, J. (2009). A Pocketful of History: Four Hundred Years of America--One State Quarter at a Time. United States: Hachette Books
State Song Research
HAWAII STATE CHAPTER 5, EMBLEMS AND SYMBOLS, §5-10 . [L1967,c301,§2;HRS§5-10;amL1990,c215,§3
State Tree Research
HAWAII STATE CHAPTER 5, §5-8 tState tree, .[L1959,JR3,§1;Supp,§14-5.2;HRS§5-8]
Twenty Interesting Facts Research
Paradise, T. R. (1998). Atlas of Hawai'i. United Kingdom: University of Hawaii Press.
Rand McNally Road Atlas 2022: Large Scale : United States. (2021). United States: Rand McNally.
Kahoòlawe Island: Restoring a Cultural Treasure : Final Report of the Kahoòlawe Island Conveyance Commission to the Congress of the United States. (1993). United States: The Commission.
Goldsberry, U. (2010). A is for Aloha: A Hawai'i Alphabet. United States: Sleeping Bear Press.
 North American Time Zones and Greenwich Mean Time (GMT).. (n.d.). (n.p.): Atmospheric Sciences Division (ATM), National Science Foundation (NSF).
Lucier, J. L. (2008). Let's Go Hawaii 5th Edition. United States: St. Martin's Press.
Fodor's. (2007). Fodor's Big Island of Hawaii. United Kingdom: Fodor's Travel Publications.
Fodor's Big Island of Hawai'i. (2010). United Kingdom: Fodor's Travel Publications.
Catalogue of the Active Volcanoes of the World: Hawaiian Islands, by G. A. Macdonald. (1956). Italy: (n.p.).
Hawaii's Story. (1898). United States: Lee and Shepard.
Joesting, E. (1988). Kauai: The Separate Kingdom. United States: University of Hawaii Press.
Ball, S. M. (1999). The Hikers Guide to the Hawaiian Islands. United States: University of Hawaii Press.
Coral Reef Remote Sensing: A Guide for Mapping, Monitoring and Management. (2013). Germany: Springer Netherlands.
Pukui, M. K., Curtis, C. (1997). Tales of the Menehune. (n.p.): Turtleback.
Ward, G. (2001). Hawaii. United Kingdom: Rough Guides.
Brackett, J. (2022). Hiking Waterfalls Hawaii: A Guide to the State's Best Waterfall Hikes. United States: Falcon Guides.
Fryklund, B. (2011). Hawaii: The Big Island. United States: Hunter Publishing, Incorporated.
Kipfer, B. A. (2008). The Order of Things. United States: Workman Publishing Company.
General Knowledge for History, Politics & Geography (Concepts + MCQs- Useful for SSC(CGL, CPO, CHSL & MTS) Railway(NTPC& Group"D"), Banking(IBPS & Bank PO), LIC, ESI and Other State Level Exams. (2023). (n.p.): SUDARSHAN PUBLICATIONS HOUSE.
Extreme Environmental Events: Complexity in Forecasting and Early Warning. (2010). Netherlands: Springer.
Ward, G. (2001). Hawaii. United Kingdom: Rough Guides.
Nemerov, A. (2017). Summoning Pearl Harbor. United States: David Zwirner Books.
Ellis, A. J. (1919). Geology and Ground Waters of the Western Part of San Diego County, California. United States: U.S. Government Printing Office.
Ten Crazy Laws

# AMERICA THE BOLD, AMERICA THE BRAVE, AMERICA THE BEAUTIFUL

State of Hawaii; [CHAPTER 302H], HAWAIIAN LANGUAGE MEDIUM EDUCATION, [§302H-1] Hawaiian language medium education program; established, [L 2004, c 133, pt of §2]
State of Hawaii; CHAPTER 165 HAWAII RIGHT TO FARM ACT, §165-4 Right to farm, [L 1982, c 256, pt of §1; am L 1986, c 242, §3; am L 2001, c 26, §2]
Maui County, Code of Ordinances; Title 9 - PUBLIC PEACE, MORALS AND WELFARE, Chapter 9.12 - PINBALL MACHINES, 9.12.010 - Unlawful for minors., (Prior code §§ 22-6.1, 22-6.2)
State of Hawaii; [CHAPTER 194}, INVASIVE SPECIES COUNCIL] §141-3. [194-2(a)]. [L 2003, c 85, §2; am L 2004, c 10, §16; am L 2006, c 109, §2]
State of Hawaii; SESSION LAWSOFHAWAII, PASSED BY THETHIRTIETH STATE LEGISLATURESTATE OF HAWAII, REGULAR SESSION2019 SESSION LAWS SLH2019
State of Hawaii; A BILL FOR AN ACT, RELATING TO FERAL CHICKEN MANAGEMENT.SECTION 1. (a)
State of Hawaii; TITLE 16. INTOXICATING LIQUOR, CHAPTER 281 INTOXICATING LIQUOR [§281-5] Powdered alcohol. [L 2015, c 186, §1]
Maui County, Hawaii; Title 9 - PUBLIC PEACE, MORALS AND WELFARE, Chapter 9.24 - CURFEW, 9.24.020 - Designated, (Ord. 1780 § 1, 1988: prior code § 22-13.2)
State of Hawaii; Haw. Rev. Stat. § 188-40, HRS § 188-40 L 1999, c 85, §§12, 17; L 2002, c 151, §1.
State of Hawaii; [CHAPTER 319 DENTAL EDUCATION], §319-3 Hawaii dental education plan., [L 1976, c 132, pt of §2; gen ch 1985; am L 1987, c 339, §4]

Idaho

Date of Statehood
Stienecker, D. L. (1996). First Facts about The States. United States: Scholastic
Rank of Admission
Stienecker, D. L. (1996). First Facts about The States. United States: Scholastic
State Capital
Aylesworth, T. G. (1990). State Capitals. United States: Gallery Books
State Capitol Building Architects
Goodsell, C. T. (2001). The American statehouse : interpreting democracy's temples. United Kingdom: University Press of Kansas
Population 2020
U.S Department of Commerce, United States Census Bureau (2020) Population and Housing State Data
Land Mass
U.S Department of Commerce, United States Census Bureau (2020) Population and Housing State Data;
Highest Record Temperature
Burt, C. C., Stroud, M. (2004). Extreme Weather: A Guide & Record Book. United Kingdom: W.W. Norton
Lowest Record Temperature
Burt, C. C., Stroud, M. (2004). Extreme Weather: A Guide & Record Book. United Kingdom: W.W. Norton.
Record Snowfall
National Oceanic and Atmospheric Adminstration, National Centers for Environmental Information {2020}: Snowfall Extremes
Record Precipitation
Burt, C. C., Stroud, M. (2004). Extreme Weather: A Guide & Record Book. United Kingdom: W.W. Norton.
Major Earthquake
Reaveley, L. D. (1985). The Borah Peak, Idaho, Earthquake of October 28, 1983. United States: (n.p.);
State Name Origin

Shearer, B. F., Shearer, B. S. (2001). State Names, Seals, Flags, and Symbols: A Historical Guide. United States: ABC-CLIO
State Nicknames
Shearer, B. F., Shearer, B. S. (2001). State Names, Seals, Flags, and Symbols: A Historical Guide. United States: ABC-CLIO;
State Slogan
Shearer, B. F., Shearer, B. S. (2001). State Names, Seals, Flags, and Symbols: A Historical Guide. United States: ABC-CLIO
State Motto
TITLE 59 PUBLIC OFFICERS IN GENERAL CHAPTER 10 MISCELLANEOUS PROVISIONS SECTION 59-1005 GREAT SEAL OF STATE
State Bird Research
TITLE 67, STATE GOVERNMENT AND STATE AFFAIRS, CHAPTER 4567-4501. STATE BIRD DESIGNATED.
State Flag Illustration
"ST Abode Stock.com" Stock photos, royalty-free images,graphics,vectors,&videos
State Flag Research
TITLE 46. MILITIA AND MILITARY AFFAIRS.CHAPTER 8. MISCELLANEOUS AND GENERAL PROVISIONS. 46-801. STATE FLAG.
State Flower Research
Idaho Statutes TITLE 67, STATE GOVERNMENT AND STATE AFFAIRS, CHAPTER 45 67-4502. STATE FLOWER DESIGNATED
State Quarter Illustration
"ST Abode Stock.com" Stock photos, royalty-free images,graphics,vectors,&videos
State Quarter Research
Noles, J. (2009). A Pocketful of History: Four Hundred Years of America--One State Quarter at a Time. United States: Hachette Books
State Song Research
TITLE 67, STATE GOVERNMENT AND STATE AFFAIRS CHAPTER 45, STATE SYMBOLS SECTION 03 67-4503. STATE SONG DESIGNATED
State Tree Research
TITLE 67 STATE GOVERNMENT AND STATE AFFAIRS CHAPTER 45 67-4504. STATE TREE DESIGNATED.
Twenty Interesting Facts Research
Reauthorization of the Intermodal Surface Transportation Efficiency Act: Hearing Before the Subcommittee on Transportation and Infrastructure of the Committee on Environment and Public Works, United States Senate, One Hundred Fifth Congress, First. (1999). United States: U.S. Government Printing Office.
Teton Dam Disaster: Hearings Before a Subcommittee of the Committee on Government Operations, House of Representatives, Ninety-fourth Congress, Second Session, August 5, 6, and 31, 1976. (1976). United States: U.S. Government Printing Office.
Backpacking Idaho: A Guide to the State's Best Backpacking Adventures. (2015). United States: Falcon Guides.
Dworshak Dam and Reservoir, North Fork Clearwater River: Environmental Impact Statement. (1975). United States: (n.p.).
Wallowa-Whitman National Forest (N.F.), Hells Canyon National Recreation Area (N.R.A.) Comprehensive Management Plan, Baker County, Wallowa County: Environmental Impact Statement. (1996). United States: (n.p.).
Idaho Wildlife. (1985). United States: Department of Fish and Game..
Hendricks, N. (2022). State Oddities: An Encyclopedia of What Makes Our United States Unique. United States: Bloomsbury Publishing.
Helman, A. (2005). The Finest Peaks: Prominence and Other Mountain Measures. United States: Trafford Publishing.
Clark, E. E. (2003). Indian Legends of the Pacific Northwest. United Kingdom: University of

California Press.
Proceedings. (1976). United States: U.S. Government Printing Office.
Edgar, S. G. (2015). What's Great about Idaho?. United States: Lerner Publishing Group.
12. Beckwith, J. A. (1972). Gem Minerals of Idaho. United States: Caxton Printers.
13. Geothermal Resources: Idaho Falls, Idaho; August 10, 1973, Klamath Falls, Oreg.; August 11, 1973. (1974). United States: U.S. Government Printing Office.
14. Hofer, C. C. (2023). New Year. United States: Capstone.
15. Plumb, G. (2013). Waterfall Lover's Guide Pacific Northwest: Where to Find Hundreds of Spectacular Waterfalls in Washington, Oregon, and Idaho, 5th Edition. United States: Mountaineers Books.
16. Alvarez, G. E., Woolford, D. (2009). Farragut Naval Training Station. United States: Arcadia Publishing.
17. Bingham, R. T. (1987). Proceedings, National Wilderness Research Conference: Issues, State-of-knowledge, Future Directions, Fort Collins, CO, July 23-26, 1985. United States: U.S. Department of Agriculture, Forest Service, Intermountain Forest and Range Experiment Station.
18. Helman, A. (2005). The Finest Peaks: Prominence and Other Mountain Measures. United States: Trafford Publishing.
19. Frank Church - River of No Return Wilderness: Management Plan. (1985). United States: U.S. Department of Agriculture, Forest Service.
20. Douglas, E. M. (1932). Boundaries, Areas, Geographic Centers and Altitudes of the United States and Their Several States: With a Brief Record of Important Changes in Their Territory and Government. United States: U.S. Government Printing Office.

Ten Crazy Laws
Town of Aberdeen, Code of Ordinances; Chapter 4 - PUBLIC HEALTH AND SAFETY, ARTICLE 4-3. - NOISE, Sec. 4-3-1. - Noises creating public disturbance, (Ord. 260, 8-12-2003)
Jefferson County, Code of Ordinances; Chapter 106 - FLOOD DAMAGE PREVENTION Sec. 106-5. - Provisions for flood hazard reduction. (b) Construction standards.(b)Construction standards. (Ord. No. 16-03, § 5, 1-25-2016)
City of Kuna, Code of Ordinances; TITLE 11 - MOTOR VEHICLES AND TRAFFIC CHAPTER 1 - GENERAL TRAFFIC PROVISIONS, 11-1-10: - RIDING HORSE AT NIGHT, LIGHT REQUIRED: (Ord., 11-1965)
City of Homedale, Code of Ordinances; Title 9 - PUBLIC PEACE, MORALS AND WELFARE, Chapter 9.16 - BB GUNS AND AIR GUNS, 9.16.010 - Discharge prohibited where. (Ord. 90 §1, 1954).
Idaho State Constitution; CHAPTER 58, PUBLIC HEALTH AND SAFETY, TITLE 18 CRIMES AND PUNISHMENTS, 18-5810. BLIND PERSONS ONLY MAY USE WHITE OR RED AND WHITE CANES, [18-5810, added 1972, ch. 336, sec. 1, p. 956.]
City of Eagle, Code of Ordinances; Ordinance 1, 5-24-1971, 5-2-2: SWEEPING DEBRIS INTO STREETS:
City of Soda Springs, Code of Ordinances; Title 9 - PUBLIC PEACE, MORALS AND WELFARE[1], Chapter 9.04 - RADIO AND TELEVISION INTERFERENCE, (Prior code §4-6-1).
Town of Notus, Code of Ordinances; Title 4 - HEALTH AND SANITATION, CHAPTER 1. - PUBLIC NUISANCES 4-1-4: - SPECIFIC NUISANCES (2007 Code)
Nez Perce County, Code of Ordinances; Sec. 5.04.080. - Title 5 - BUSINESS LICENSES AND REGULATIONS, CHAPTER 5.01. - IN GENERAL CHAPTER 5.04. - ALCOHOLIC BEVERAGE SALES Reasons for denial of license, (Code 1997, § 5.04.080; Ord. No. 51b, § 8, 1993)
Idaho State 105th Legislative; General Laws of the State of Idaho, Chapter 65 H.B., #214, Section 14.

## Illinois

Date of Statehood
Stienecker, D. L. (1996). First Facts about The States. United States: Scholastic
Rank of Admission

Stienecker, D. L. (1996). First Facts about The States. United States: Scholastic
State Capital
Aylesworth, T. G. (1990). State Capitals. United States: Gallery Books;
State Capitol Building Architects
Goodsell, C. T. (2001). The American statehouse : interpreting democracy's temples. United Kingdom: University Press of Kansas
Population 2020
U.S Department of Commerce, United States Census Bureau (2020) Population and Housing State Data
Land Mass
U.S Department of Commerce, United States Census Bureau (2020) Population and Housing State Data
Highest Record Temperature
Burt, C. C., Stroud, M. (2004). Extreme Weather: A Guide & Record Book. United Kingdom: W.W. Norton.
Lowest Record Temperature
Burt, C. C., Stroud, M. (2004). Extreme Weather: A Guide & Record Book. United Kingdom: W.W. Norton.
Record Snowfall
Burt, C. C., Stroud, M. (2004). Extreme Weather: A Guide & Record Book. United Kingdom: W.W. Norton.
Record Precipitation
Burt, C. C., Stroud, M. (2004). Extreme Weather: A Guide & Record Book. United Kingdom: W.W. Norton.
Major Earthquake
Final Report of the Illinois Seismic Safety Task Force. (2011). United States: Illinois Department of Insurance
State Name Origin
Shearer, B. F., Shearer, B. S. (2001). State Names, Seals, Flags, and Symbols: A Historical Guide. United States: ABC-CLIO
State Nicknames
Shearer, B. F., Shearer, B. S. (2001). State Names, Seals, Flags, and Symbols: A Historical Guide. United States: ABC-CLIO;
State Slogan
Shearer, B. F., Shearer, B. S. (2001). State Names, Seals, Flags, and Symbols: A Historical Guide. United States: ABC-CLIO
State Motto
GOVERNMENT. CHAPTER 5 GENERAL PROVISIONS. (5 ILCS 460/) State Designations Act. (5 ILCS 460/5)
State Bird Research
GENERAL PROVISIONS (5 ILCS 460/) State Designations Act.(5 ILCS 460/10) (from Ch. 1, par. 2901-10) Sec. 10. State bird.
State Flag Illustration
"ST Abode Stock.com" Stock photos, royalty-free images,graphics,vectors,&videos; Retrieved Jun 17,2022
State Flag Research
CHAPTER 5 - GENERAL PROVISIONS. (5 ILCS 460/) State Designations Act.
(5 ILCS 460/5) (from Ch. 1, par. 2901-5), Sec. 5
State Flower Research
GOVERNMENT CHAPTER 5. GENERAL PROVISIONS. (5 ILCS 460/) State Designations Act. (5 ILCS 460/40) (from Ch. 1, par. 2901-40) Sec. 40
State Quarter Illustration
"ST Abode Stock.com" Stock photos, royalty-free images,graphics,vectors,&videos; Retrieved Jun 21,2022

State Quarter Research
Noles, J. (2009). A Pocketful of History: Four Hundred Years of America--One State Quarter at a Time. United States: Hachette Books; Retrieved May 14,2021
State Song Research
GENERAL PROVISIONS STATE DESIGNATIONS ACT SECTION 35
State Tree Research
CHAPTER 5. GENERAL PROVISIONS. STATE DESIGNATIONS. (5 ILCS 460/40) (from Ch. 1, par. 2901-40) Sec. 40
Twenty Interesting Facts Research
Miller, R. (2000). The Great Chicago Fire. United States: University of Illinois Press.
Illinois and Mississippi Rivers, and Diversion of Water from Lake Michigan: Hearings on the Subject of the Improvement of the Illinois and Mississippi Rivers, and the Diversion of Water from Lake Michigan Into the Illinois River Held Before the Committee on Rivers and Harbors, House of Representatives, Sixty-eighth Congress, First Session. (1924). United States: U.S. Government Printing Office.
Lanyon, R. (1999). "So They Reversed the River": A History of the Construction of the Main Channel and Improvements to the Chicago and Des Plaines Rivers from 1892 to 1900 for the Reversal of the Chicago River. United States: Richard Lanyon.
Moreno, R. (2011). Illinois Curiosities: Quirky Characters, Roadside Oddities & Other Offbeat Stuff. United States: Globe Pequot.
H.R. 714, the Illinois Land Conservation Act of 1995: Hearing Before the Committee on Transportation and Infrastructure, House of Representatives, One Hundred Fourth Congress, First Session, April 17, 1995. (1995). United States: U.S. Government Printing Office.
Wilton, D. (2008). Word Myths: Debunking Linguistic Urban Legends. United States: Oxford University Press.
Shawnee National Forest (N.F.), Land and Resource(s) Management Plan (LRMP): Environmental Impact Statement. (1986). United States: (n.p.).
of Architects Chicago, A. I. (2014). AIA Guide to Chicago. United States: University of Illinois Press.
Naden, C. J. (1968). The Haymarket Affair, Chicago, 1886: The "great Anarchist" Riot and Trial. United States: Watts.
Zoellner, T. (2021). The National Road: Dispatches from a Changing America. United States: Catapult.
Genzen, J. (2007). The Chicago River: A History in Photographs. United States: Westcliffe Publishers.
Hanley, M. (2012). True Tales of Aurora, Illinois: Mysterious Murders, Presidential Visits and Blues Legends in the City of Lights. United States: Arcadia Publishing Incorporated.
Taylor, T., Moran, M., Sceurman, M. (2005). Weird Illinois: Your Travel Guide to Illinois' Local Legends and Best Kept Secrets. United States: Sterling.
Carlyle Lake Project, Kaskaskia Valley: Environmental Impact Statement. (1974). United States: (n.p.).
Kaskaskia River, Illinois. (1958). United States: U.S. Government Printing Office.
Illinois Geographic Names. (1981). United States: U.S.G.S. Topographic Division, Office of Research & Technical Standards, National Center.
Local Government Structure in the United States. (1954). United States: U.S. Government Printing Office.
Zimmerman OFM, J. (2023). Cura Animarum: The Sacred Heart Province of the Order of Friars Minor in North America: 1858–2023. United States: iUniverse.
Our Chicago. (n.d.). (n.p.): Voyageur Press.
The Chicago World's Fair of 1893: A Photographic Record. (2012). United States: Dover Publications.
Rothert, O. A. (2022). The Outlaws of Cave-in-Rock: Historical Accounts of the Famous Highwaymen and River Pirates. Czechia: DigiCat.
Ten Crazy Laws

City of Chicago, Code of Ordinances; Chapter 8 - BARBERS AND BEAUTY CULTURE[1], ARTICLE III. - PRACTICE OF BEAUTY CULTURE Sec. 8-31. - Practice defined, (Ord. of 7-29-68, § 9.5)
City of Perioa, Code of Ordinances; Chapter 20 - GARBAGE AND TRASH, ARTICLE I. - IN GENERAL, Sec. 20-17. - Separate containers required, (Code 1954, § 18.3; Ord. No. Mis-92-5, § 3, 4-6-92)
Village of Crete, Code of Ordinances; Chapter 25 - TRAFFIC, ARTICLE I. - IN GENERAL, Sec. 25-12. - Registration and regulation of bicycles, (Ord. No. 858, § 1(4.5.2), 9-27-82; Ord. No. 86-13A, § 1, 1-5-87)
Chapter 5 - ANIMALS AND FOWL[1} ARTICLE I. - IN GENERAL Sec. 5-7. - Cruelty to animals. (Ord. No. 79-4-1, § 7, 4-2-79; Ord. No. 2001-1-2, § I, 1-22-2001)
Town of Des Plaines , Code of Ordinances; CHAPTER 3 STOPPING, STANDING AND PARKING 7-3-7: PEDESTRIAN STANDING ON SIDEWALK:
City of Normal, Code of Ordinances; DIVISION 17.8 - ANIMALS, 17.8-2 DANGEROUS ANIMALS, (Sec. 17.8-2.5 Added 10/6/2014 by Ord. No. 5559)
State of Illinois, 720 ILCS 5/26-6 Sec. 26-6. Disorderly conduct at a funeral or memorial service.
Village of Sleepy Hollow, Code of Ordinances; CHAPTER 7 - PLEASURE DRIVEWAYS Sec. 6-7-2. - General regulations (Ord. 2013-3, 2-4-2013)
City of Forsyth, Code of Ordinances; CHAPTER 92. - NUISANCES DIVISION 2. - PUBLIC NUISANCES Sec. 92.19. - Weed/grass control and nuisance trees (Prior code, § 92.14; Ord. No. 373, 9-25-1991; Ord. No. 2016-4, 4-4-2016)
CHAPTER 2 - MISCELLANEOUS OFFENSES 6-2-1: - OBSTRUCTING AUTHORITY: (1975 Code §§ 19-2, 19-3; amd. 2003 Code)

## Indiana

Date of Statehood
Stienecker, D. L. (1996). First Facts about The States. United States: Scholastic
Rank of Admission
Stienecker, D. L. (1996). First Facts about The States. United States: Scholastic
State Capital
Aylesworth, T. G. (1990). State Capitals. United States: Gallery Books
State Capitol Building Architects
Elliott, C. D. (2003). The American Architect from the Colonial Era to the Present. United Kingdom: McFarland, Incorporated, Publishers
Population 2020
U.S Department of Commerce, United States Census Bureau (2020) Population and Housing State Data
Land Mass
U.S Department of Commerce, United States Census Bureau (2020) Population and Housing State Data
Highest Record Temperature
Burt, C. C., Stroud, M. (2004). Extreme Weather: A Guide & Record Book. United Kingdom: W.W. Norton.
Lowest Record Temperature
Burt, C. C., Stroud, M. (2004). Extreme Weather: A Guide & Record Book. United Kingdom: W.W. Norton
Record Snowfall
National Oceanic and Atmospheric Adminstration, National Centers for Environmental Information {2020}: Snowfall Extremes
Record Precipitation
Burt, C. C., Stroud, M. (2004). Extreme Weather: A Guide & Record Book. United Kingdom: W.W. Norton.
Major Earthquake

Earthquake History of the United States. (1982). United States: U.S. Department of Commerce, National Oceanic and Atmospheric Administration and U.S. Department of the Interior, Geological Survey;.
State Name Origin
Shearer, B. F., Shearer, B. S. (2001). State Names, Seals, Flags, and Symbols: A Historical Guide. United States: ABC-CLIO
State Nicknames
Shearer, B. F., Shearer, B. S. (2001). State Names, Seals, Flags, and Symbols: A Historical Guide. United States: ABC-CLIO
State Slogan
Shearer, B. F., Shearer, B. S. (2001). State Names, Seals, Flags, and Symbols: A Historical Guide. United States: ABC-CLIO
State Motto
Eightieth Session of the General Assembly, Joint Resolution No 6. March 2, 1937
State Bird Research
TITLE 1. GENERAL PROVISIONS. ARTICLE 2. STATE EMBLEMS. CHAPTER 8. STATE BIRD.
IC 1-2-8-1 Cardinal.(Formerly: Acts 1933, c.223, s.1.)
State Flag Illustration
"ST Abode Stock.com" Stock photos, royalty-free images,graphics,vectors,&videos; https://bit.ly/3P9x0Ee
State Flag Research
TITLE 1. GENERAL PROVISIONS. ARTICLE 2. STATE EMBLEMS. CHAPTER 2. STATE FLAG.
IC 1-2-2-1 (Formerly: Acts 1917, c.114, s.1; Acts 1955, c.146, s.1.) As amended by Acts 1979, P.L.1, SEC.1.
State Flower Research
Indiana General Assembly; Indiana Code IC 1-2-7-1Sec. 1. (Formerly: Acts 1931, c.48, s.1; Acts 1957, c.283, s.1.)
Peribology. (n.d.). (n.p.): (n.p.).
State Quarter Illustration
"ST Abode Stock.com" Stock photos, royalty-free images,graphics,vectors,&videos; https://bit.ly/3FzE6Pl
State Quarter Research
Noles, J. (2009). A Pocketful of History: Four Hundred Years of America--One State Quarter at a Time. United States: Hachette Books
State Song Research
TITLE 1. GENERAL PROVISIONS ARTICLE 2. STATE EMBLEMS CHAPTER 6. STATE SONG SECTION 1(Formerly: Acts 1913, c.254, s.1.)
State Tree Research
TITLE 1. GENERAL PROVISIONS. ARTICLE 2. STATE EMBLEMS. CHAPTER 7. STATE FLOWER AND TREE. SECTION IC 1-2-7-1. IC 1-2-7-1 Tulip tree; peony(Formerly: Acts 1931, c.48, s.1; Acts 1957, c.283, s.1.)
Twenty Interesting Facts Research
Dill, M. (2020). The Legend of the First Super Speedway: The Battle for the Soul of American Auto Racing. (n.p.): BookBaby.
Hartemann, F., Hauptman, R. (2005). The Mountain Encyclopedia: An A to Z Compendium of Over 2,250 Terms, Concepts, Ideas, and People. United States: Taylor Trade Publishing.
Frushour, S. S. (2012). A Guide to Caves and Karst of Indiana. United States: Indiana University Press.
Elves, T. (2015). Letters to Santa Claus. United States: Indiana University Press.
Lomax, E., Garceau, A. V. (2014). Syracuse and Lake Wawasee. United States: Arcadia Publishing.
Blatchley, W. S., Ashley, G. H. (1901). The Lakes of Northern Indiana and Their Associated Marl Deposits. United States: Department of Geology and Natural Resources.
Indiana Lake Michigan Coastal Program: Environmental Impact Statement. (2002). United States: (n.p.).

Dickinson, R. (2017). The Notorious Reno Gang: The Wild Story of the West's First Brotherhood of Thieves, Assassins, and Train Robbers. United States: Lyons Press.
Maumee River Basin Water and Related Land Resources: Report - Environmental Impact Statement. (1977). United States: Great Lakes Basin Commission.
Winger, O. (1935). A Brief Centennial History of Wabash County, 1835-1935. United States: (n.p.).
Lytle, R. M. (2015). The Great Circus Train Wreck of 1918: Tragedy on the Indiana Lakeshore. United States: Arcadia Publishing.
Institute, B. R. (2012). Uncle John's Fully Loaded: 25th Anniversary Bathroom Reader. United States: Printers Row.
Habitats and Ecological Communities of Indiana: Presettlement to Present. (2012). Ukraine: Indiana University Press.
Farnsley, A. E., Farnsley, A. E., Demerath III, N. J., Diamond, E., Mapes, M. L. (2005). Sacred Circles, Public Squares: The Multicentering of American Religion. Ukraine: Indiana University Press.
The Encyclopedia of Indianapolis. (1994). United States: Indiana University Press.
Studies in Indiana Geography. (1897). United States: Inland Publishing Company.
Partlow, G. (2014). America's Deadliest Twister: The Tri-State Tornado of 1925. United States: Southern Illinois University Press.
16. The Encyclopedia of Indianapolis. (1994). United States: Indiana University Press.
Lincoln Boyhood National Memorial (N.M), General Management Plan: Environmental Impact Statement. (2005). United States: (n.p.).
Laws Relating to the National Park Service: Supplement .... (1974). United States: U.S. Government Printing Office.
Travel Guides, F. (2021). Fodor's The Complete Guide to the National Parks of the USA: All 63 Parks from Maine to American Samoa. United States: Fodor's Travel.
Ferrucci, K. (2004). Limestone Lives: Voices from the Indiana Stone Belt. United States: Quarry Books.
Douglas, E. M. (1939). Boundaries, Areas, Geographic Centers and Altitudes of the United States and Their Several States: With a Brief Record of Important Changes in Their Territory and Government. United States: U.S. Government Printing Office.
Baker, R. L. (1984). Hoosier Folk Legends. United States: Indiana University Press.
Ten Crazy Laws
State of Indiana, 844 Ind. Admin. Code 12-5-4 844 IAC 12-5-4
City of South Bend, Code of Ordinances; ARTICLE 4. - OFFENSES AGAINST PUBLIC PEACE AND SAFETY Sec. 13-57. - Unreasonable noise. (Code 1962, § 26-15; Ord. No. 5610-73, § 1; Ord. No. 6771-80, § 1; Ord. No. 9642-05, § I, 11-28-05)
State of Indiana IC 14-22-9 2012 Indiana Code TITLE 14. NATURAL AND CULTURAL RESOURCES ARTICLE 22. FISH AND WILDLIFE Chapter 9. Regulation of Fishing IC 14-22-9-1 Unlawful means of taking fish; special permits P.L.1-1995, SEC.15. Amended by P.L.165-2011, SEC.8; P.L.151-2012, SEC.15.
City of Indianapolis, Code of Ordinances; Chapter 895 - HORSE-DRAWN CARRIAGES Sec. 895-4. - Restrictions on hours of operation, and streets.(G.O. 97, 1999, § 1; G.O. 63, 2009, § 142; G.O. 13, 2016, § 17)
County of Noble, Code of Ordinances; Chapter 18 - HEALTH ARTICLE I. - IN GENERAL DIVISION 3. - STANDARDS AND REQUIREMENTS Sec. 18-145. - Age limitation/consent.(Ord. No. 2002-5, § 4, 6-17-2002)
Chapter 54 - OFFENSES AND MISCELLANEOUS PROVISIONS ARTICLE III. - OFFENSES INVOLVING PUBLIC SAFETY Sec. 54-61. - Throwing objects across streets, alleys, sidewalks and other public places. (Code 1974, § 18-2)
City of Wabash, Code of Ordinances; ARTICLE 7. - PUBLIC AND PRIVATE NUISANCES Sec. 6-78. - Specific nuisances prohibited (Wabash City Code, § 6-79)
City of Beech Grove, Code of Ordinances; CHAPTER 115: PEDDLERS AND SOLICITORS ITINERANT FOOD PEDDLERS ;§ 115.21 LICENSE REQUIRED. ('67 Code, § 113.02) (Ord. 7-1959, passed 6-l- 59; Am. Ord. 2, 2016, passed 3-7-16)

Chapter 14 - ANIMALS
City of Wanatah, Code of Ordinances; ARTICLE I. - IN GENERAL Sec. 14-29. - Teasing and tormenting dogs/cats (Ord. No. 09-90, § 11, 10-4-1990)
DIVISION 3. - STANDARDS
City of Merrillville, Code of Ordinances; Chapter 11 - MOBILE HOMES AND MOBILE HOME PARKS[1] Sec. 11-66. - Interior streets or drives (Ord. No. 72-23, § IV(B)(1), 12-26-72)

## Iowa

Date of Statehood
Stienecker, D. L. (1996). First Facts about The States. United States: Scholastic
Rank of Admission
Stienecker, D. L. (1996). First Facts about The States. United States: Scholastic
State Capital
Aylesworth, T. G. (1990). State Capitals. United States: Gallery Books
State Capitol Building Architects
Goodsell, C. T. (2001). The American statehouse : interpreting democracy's temples. United Kingdom: University Press of Kansas
Population 2020
U.S Department of Commerce, United States Census Bureau (2020) Population and Housing State Data;
Land Mass
U.S Department of Commerce, United States Census Bureau (2020) Population and Housing State Data;
Highest Record Temperature
Burt, C. C., Stroud, M. (2004). Extreme Weather: A Guide & Record Book. United Kingdom: W.W. Norton.
Lowest Record Temperature
Burt, C. C., Stroud, M. (2004). Extreme Weather: A Guide & Record Book. United Kingdom: W.W. Norton
Record Snowfall
National Oceanic and Atmospheric Adminstration, National Centers for Environmental Information {2020}: Snowfall Extremes
Record Precipitation
Burt, C. C., Stroud, M. (2004). Extreme Weather: A Guide & Record Book. United Kingdom: W.W. Norton.
Major Earthquake
Heck, N. H., Wood, H. O., Allen, M. W. (1938). Earthquake History of the United States .... United States: U.S. Government Printing Office.
State Name Origin
Shearer, B. F., Shearer, B. S. (2001). State Names, Seals, Flags, and Symbols: A Historical Guide. United States: ABC-CLIO
State Nicknames
Shearer, B. F., Shearer, B. S. (2001). State Names, Seals, Flags, and Symbols: A Historical Guide. United States: ABC-CLIO
State Slogan
Shearer, B. F., Shearer, B. S. (2001). State Names, Seals, Flags, and Symbols: A Historical Guide. United States: ABC-CLIO
State Motto
TITLE I STATE SOVEREIGNTY AND MANAGEMENT SUBTITLE 1 SOVEREIGNTY CHAPTER 1A GREAT SEAL OF IOWA 1A.1 Seal - device - motto; [1GA, ch 112; C75, 77, 79, 81, §1A.1]
State Bird Research
Iowa Concurrent Resolution No. 22, March 22, 1933

RONDA SEXTON

State Flag Illustration
"ST Abode Stock" Stock photos, royalty-free images,graphics,vectors,&videos
https://bit.ly/3HcpYwy
State Flag Research
TITLE I. STATE SOVEREIGNTY AND MANAGEMENT. SUBTITLE 1. SOVEREIGNTY. CHAPTER 1B. STATE FLAG. 1B.1 Specifications of state flag
State Flower Research
Extra Session of the Twenty-sixth General Assembly of the State of Iowa, May 7, 1897
State Quarter Illustration
"ST Abode Stock" Stock photos, royalty-free images,graphics,vectors,&videos
https://bit.ly/3UxUl3u
State Quarter Research
Noles, J. (2009). A Pocketful of History: Four Hundred Years of America--One State Quarter at a Time. United States: Hachette Books
State Tree Research
59th Iowa General Assembly, Agriculture 2. Section 1. House Joint Resolution
a) The Bur Oak
Twenty Intersting Facts Research
1. Rice, L. R. (2009). An Exploreres Guide Iowa. United Kingdom: Countryman Press.
2. Stevens, W. B. (1921). One hundred years ago. United States: S.J. Clarke Publishing Company.
Everett, D. R. (2014). Creating the American West: Boundaries and Borderlands. United States: University of Oklahoma Press.
3. Federal Writers Project, J. F. (2010). The WPA Guide to 1930s Iowa. United States: University of Iowa Press
need more
4. Karras, J., Karras, A. (1999). RAGBRAI: Everyone Pronounces It Wrong. United States: University of Iowa Press.
5. Bannister, M. (2023). Secret Iowa: A Guide to the Weird, Wonderful, and Obscure. United States: Reedy Press.
6. Horton, L. N., Horton, L. O. (2004). Uniquely Iowa. United States: Heinemann Library.
7. Whye, M. (2001). Great Iowa Weekend Adventures. United States: Trails Books.
Brick, G. A. (2004). Iowa Underground: A Guide to the State's Subterranean Treasures. United States: Trails Books.
8. Hearings. (1963). United States: (n.p.).
Dinsmore, J. J., Dinsmore, S. J. (2023). Iowa's Changing Wildlife: Three Decades of Gain and Loss. United States: University of Iowa Press.
9. Concrete. (1927). United States: Concrete-Cement Age Publishing Company.
10. .Hartemann, F., Hauptman, R. (2005). The Mountain Encyclopedia: An A to Z Compendium of Over 2,250 Terms, Concepts, Ideas, and People. United States: Taylor Trade Publishing.
Shepard, R. C., Bitterman, P., Archer, J. C., Shelley, F. M. (2024). Atlas of Iowa. United States: University of Iowa Press.
Mississippi River Between Missouri River and Minneapolis, Minn., Damage to Levee and Drainage Districts: Letter from the Secretary of the Army Transmitting a Letter from the Chief of Engineers, United States Army, Dated November 30, 1954 ..... (1955). United States: U.S. Government Printing Office.
Bannister, M. (2023). Secret Iowa: A Guide to the Weird, Wonderful, and Obscure. United States: Reedy Press.
Iowa: 2010, Population and Housing Unit Counts, CPH-2-17, 2010 Census of Population and Housing, Issued August 2012, *. (2013). United States: (n.p.).
Pohlen, J. (2005). Oddball Iowa: A Guide to Some Really Strange Places. United States: Chicago Review Press.
Clayton, W. H. H., Elder, III, D. C. (1998). A Damned Iowa Greyhound: The Civil War Letters of William Henry Harrison Clayton. United States: University of Iowa Press.
Smith, H. I. (1903). History of the Seventh Iowa Veteran Volunteer Infantry During the Civil

War. United States: E. Hitchcock, printer.
Bremer, J. (2023). A New History of Iowa. United States: University Press of Kansas.
Wakefield, E. H. (1994). History of the Electric Automobile: Battery-only Powered Cars. United States: Society of Automotive Engineers.
Census of population and housing (2020): Iowa Population and Housing Unit Counts.
Whye, M. (2004). The Great Iowa Touring Book: 27 Spectacular Auto Tours. United States: Trails Books.
19, Brick, G. A. (2004). Iowa Underground: A Guide to the State's Subterranean Treasures. United States: Trails Books.
Stock, J. B. (2003). Amazing Iowa. United States: HarperCollins Christian Publishing.
Trask, K. A. (2006). Black Hawk: The Battle for the Heart of America. United States: Henry Holt and Company.
Ten Crazy Laws
City of Ottumwa, Code of Ordinances; Chapter 25 - PUBLIC OFFENSES ARTICLE IV. - SPECIFIC OFFENSES Sec. 25-67. - Barbed wire Code 1970, § 25-23; Ord. No. 2352, § 25, 1-25-1978; Ord. No. 2703, § 1, 12-20-1988)
City of Keokuk, Code of Ordinances; Title 8 - PEACE, SAFETY AND MORALS Chapter 8.09 - USE OF THE WATERFRONT 8.09.010 - Tying to over twenty-four hours prohibited (Ord. 1374 § 1 (part), 1983)City of Mount Vernon, City Ordinances; CHAPTER 47 PARK REGULATIONS 47.01   TREES AND FLOWERS.
Iowa Constitution; TITLE V AGRICULTURE SUBTITLE 4 AGRICULTURE-RELATED PRODUCTS AND ACTIVITIES CHAPTER 210 STANDARD WEIGHTS AND MEASURES 210.14Hop boxes.
City of Algona, Code of Ordinances;  Title 9 - PUBLIC PEACE, MORALS AND WELFARE 9.04.060 - False alarms (Prior code § 2.1-1.0405)
City of Wilton, Code of Ordinances; Chapter 9.16 - MISCELLANEOUS OFFENSES 9.16.070 - Noise (Ord. 190 §1(6), 1973).
City of Decorah, Code of Ordinances; Title 6 - ANIMALS 6.12.010 - Bothersome animals (Amended during 1976 codification: prior code § 15.1(32))(Ord. No. 1213, § 2, 12-4-2017)
Chapter 25 - PUBLIC OFFENSES ARTICLE IV. - SPECIFIC OFFENSES Sec. 25-70. - Harassment (Code 1970, § 25-26; Ord. No. 2352, § 25, 1-25-1978)
City of Cedar Rapids, Code of Ordinances;  CHAPTER 10 - PARKS AND PUBLIC PLACES 10.07 - TREES IN PUBLIC PLACES (d)Placing Materials Near Trees.
Chapter 14 - AMUSEMENTS AND ENTERTAINMENTS ARTICLE V. - AMUSEMENT HOUSES Sec. 14-155. - Building standards and inspections (C85, § 6-99; O.11,393, 11,526; C91, § 6-99; O.13,011)

Kansas

Date of Statehood
Stienecker, D. L. (1996). First Facts about The States. United States: Scholastic
Rank of Admission
Stienecker, D. L. (1996). First Facts about The States. United States: Scholastic
State Capital
Aylesworth, T. G. (1990). State Capitals. United States: Gallery Books
State Capitol Building Architect(s)
Goodsell, C. T. (2001). The American statehouse : interpreting democracy's temples. United Kingdom: University Press of Kansas
Population 2020
U.S Department of Commerce, United States Census Bureau (2020) Population and Housing State Data
Land Mass
U.S Department of Commerce, United States Census Bureau (2020) Population and Housing State Data

Highest Record Temperature
Burt, C. C., Stroud, M. (2004). Extreme Weather: A Guide & Record Book. United Kingdom: W.W. Norton.
Lowest Record Temperature
Burt, C. C., Stroud, M. (2004). Extreme Weather: A Guide & Record Book. United Kingdom: W.W. Norton.
Record Snowfall
National Oceanic and Atmospheric Adminstration, National Centers for Environmental Information {2020}: Snowfall Extremes
Record Precipitation
Burt, C. C., Stroud, M. (2004). Extreme Weather: A Guide & Record Book. United Kingdom: W.W. Norton.
Major Earthquake
NUREG/CR.. (1978). United States: U.S. Nuclear Regulatory Commission
State Name Origin
Shearer, B. F., Shearer, B. S. (2001). State Names, Seals, Flags, and Symbols: A Historical Guide. United States: ABC-CLIO
State Nicknames
Shearer, B. F., Shearer, B. S. (2001). State Names, Seals, Flags, and Symbols: A Historical Guide. United States: ABC-CLIO
State Slogan
Shearer, B. F., Shearer, B. S. (2001). State Names, Seals, Flags, and Symbols: A Historical Guide. United States: ABC-CLIO
State Motto
CHAPTER 75. STATE DEPARTMENTS; PUBLIC OFFICERS AND EMPLOYEES. ARTICLE 2. STATE SEAL 75-201. Great seal of the state of Kansas.History: L. 1879, ch. 166, § 15; March 20; R.S. 1923, 75-201
State Bird Research
Chapter 73.--SOLDIERS, SAILORS AND PATRIOTIC EMBLEMS. Article 9.--STATE BIRD. 73-901. Designation, History: L. 1937, ch. 319, § 1; June 30.;
State Flag Illustration
"ST Abode Stock.com" Stock photos, royalty-free images,graphics,vectors,&videos; https://bit.ly/3VVdehS
State Flag Research
Chapter 73. - SOLDIERS, SAILORS AND PATRIOTIC EMBLEMS. Article 7. - FLAG AND PATRIOTIC EMBLEMS. 73-701. State flag.History: L. 1927, ch. 281, § 1; March 23;
State Flower Research
Chapter 73.--SOLDIERS, SAILORS AND PATRIOTIC EMBLEMS. Article 18.--STATE FLOWER AND FLORAL EMBLEM. SECTION 73-1801. 73-1801. State flower and floral emblem, History: L. 1903, ch. 479, § 1; June 1; R.S. 1923, 75-3033;
State Quarter Illustration
"ST Abode Stock.com" Stock photos, royalty-free images,graphics,vectors,&videos; https://bit.ly/3W1K9RM
State Quarter Research
Noles, J. (2009). A Pocketful of History: Four Hundred Years of America--One State Quarter at a Time. United States: Hachette Books;
State Song Research
Chapter 73.--SOLDIERS, SAILORS AND PATRIOTIC EMBLEMS Article 13.--STATE SONG SECTION 01 73-1301.History: L. 1947, ch. 433, § 1; June 30;
State Tree Research
Kansas House Bill No. 113 Chapter 318 Designating the Cottonwood Tree as the official state tree;
Twenty Interesting Facts Research
1. Frazier, G. (2017). The Last Wild Places of Kansas: Journeys Into Hidden Landscapes. United States: University Press of Kansas.

2. Flora, S. D. (1948). Climate of Kansas. United States: Kansas State Board of Agriculture.
3. Brackman, B. (1997). Kansas Trivia. United States: Thomas Nelson.
4. Harmetz, A. (2013). The Making of The Wizard of Oz. United States: Chicago Review Press, Incorporated.
5. Grout, P. (2010). Kansas Curiosities: Quirky Characters, Roadside Oddities & Other Offbeat Stuff. United States: Globe Pequot.
6. Davis, K. S. (1984). Kansas: A History. United States: W. W. Norton.
7. Conard, J., Conard, K. M. (2015). Kansas Trail Guide: The Best Hiking, Biking, and Riding in the Sunflower State. United States: University Press of Kansas.
8. Meister, C. (1999). Tornadoes. United States: ABDO Publishing Company.
Fradin, J. B., Fradin, D. B. (2011). Tornado! The Story Behind These Twisting, Turning, Spinning, and Spiraling Storms. United States: National Geographic.
9. Arkansas River Navigation Study, Little Rock and Tulsa Districts: Environmental Impact Statement. (2005). United States: (n.p.).
10, Meyer, D. L. (2017). Kansas Myths and Legends: The True Stories Behind History's Mysteries. United States: Globe Pequot.
11. Kowtko, S. (2009). America's Natural Places: [5 Volumes]. United States: ABC-CLIO.
12. Mine Disasters. (2000). United States: U.S. Department of Labor, Mine Safety and Health Administration, National Mine Health and Safety Academy.
McIntosh, R. E. (1918). Kansas Mining Laws and Laws Especially Affecting the Employment of Labor in Mines (annotated), Compiled for State Department of Labor and Industry. United States: W.R. Smith.
13. Junction City & Geary County Kansas Fishing & Floating Guide Book: Complete fishing and floating information for Geary County Kansas. (2016). (n.p.): Recreational Guides.
14 Kowtko, S. (2009). America's Natural Places: [5 Volumes]. United States: ABC-CLIO.
15, Ecology. (1926). United States: Ecological Society of America.
King, D. C. (2004). Kansas. United States: Benchmark Books/Marshall Cavendish.
16. Endangered Species Technical Bulletin. (1994). United States: The Program.
Johnsgard, P. A. (2018). A Naturalist's Guide to the Great Plains: Sites, Species, and Spectacles. United States: Zea Books.
17. Mason, R. (2002). Rare Visions & Roadside Revelations. United States: Kansas City Star Books.
18. Inside the Ropes: Sportswriters Get Their Game on. (2008). Ukraine: University of Nebraska Press.
Buchanan, R., McCauley, J. R. (1987). Roadside Kansas: A Traveler's Guide to Its Geology and Landmarks. United States: University Press of Kansas for the Kansas Geological Survey.
19. Marsh, C. (1994). Kansas Dingbats!. (n.p.): Gallopade International.
20. Allaby, M. (2014). Tornadoes. United States: Facts On File, Incorporated.
Ten Crazy Laws
City of Larned, Code of Ordinances; PART II - ZONING REGULATIONS,Sec. 3.60. - Application of regulations (Ord. No. 1088, exh. A(3.60, 3.61), 10-4-1982)
City of Arkansas City, Code of Ordinances; Chapter 42 - MISCELLANEOUS OFFENSES Sec. 42-28. - Air gun, air rifle, bow and arrow, slingshot, BB gun or paint ball gun; section 10.6 of the Standard Uniform Public Offense Code amended. (Ord. No. 2012-12-4321, § 1, 12-4-2012)
City of Wichita, Code of Ordinances; Title 8 - NUISANCES Sec. 8.01.055. - Nuisances (Ord. No. 47-894, § 5, 5-20-08)
City of Overland Park, Code of Ordinances; 11.28.064 Funeral Picketing. (Repealed), (History: Ord. POC-3423 §5, 2023; Ord. POC-2766 §3, 2008; POC-2605 §1, 2006; POC-1792 §1, 93)(State Law: K.S.A. 21-6106)
City of Shawnee, Code of Ordinances; TITLE 12 - STREETS, SIDEWALKS AND PUBLIC PLACES 12.12.095 - Use of Parks and Cemetery—Restrictions (Ord. 2886, 2005) (Ord. 2181, 1994)(Prior Code Section 10-110)
City of Wichita, Code of Ordinances; Title 8 - NUISANCES Sec. 8.02.060. - Notice of Chronic Nuisance (Ord. No. 50-357, § 6, 12-6-16)
City of Valley Centery, Code of Ordinances; Title 6 - ANIMAL CONTROL REGULATIONS 6.21.030 -

RONDA SEXTON

Animal regulations for A-1 and RR-1 zoning (Ord. No. 1281, § 1, 11-4-14)
City of Osage City, Code of Ordinances; Chapter 26 - OFFENSES AND MISCELLANEOUS PROVISIONS Sec. 26-2. - Loud sound amplification systems (Code 1998, §§ 8-701—8-703; Ord. No. 1330, § 1)
City of Coffeyville, Code of Ordinances; CHAPTER 8.02. - EXCESSIVE CALLS FOR POLICE SERVICE AT CHRONIC NUISANCE PROPERTIES Chapter 28 - OFFENSES ARTICLE IX. - OFFENSES AGAINST PUBLIC MORAL Sec. 28-210. - False membership claims (Code 1977, § 17-215)
City of Neodesha, Code of Ordinances; ARTICLE II. - HEALTH NUISANCES, Sec. 26-19. - Nuisances unlawful; defined (1), (Ord. No. 1739, § 1, 11-25-2020)

Kentucky

Date of Statehood
Stienecker, D. L. (1996). First Facts about The States. United States: Scholastic
Rank of Admission
Stienecker, D. L. (1996). First Facts about The States. United States: Scholastic
State Capital
Aylesworth, T. G. (1990). State Capitals. United States: Gallery Books;
State Capitol Building Architects
Goodsell, C. T. (2001). The American statehouse : interpreting democracy's temples. United Kingdom: University Press of Kansas
Population 2020
U.S Department of Commerce, United States Census Bureau (2020) Population and Housing State Data
Land Mass
U.S Department of Commerce, United States Census Bureau (2020) Population and Housing State Data
Highest Record Temperature
Burt, C. C., Stroud, M. (2004). Extreme Weather: A Guide & Record Book. United Kingdom: W.W. Norton
Lowest Record Temperature
Burt, C. C., Stroud, M. (2004). Extreme Weather: A Guide & Record Book. United Kingdom: W.W. Norton
Record Snowfall
National Oceanic and Atmospheric Adminstration, National Centers for Environmental Information {2020}: Snowfall Extremes
Record Precipitation
Burt, C. C., Stroud, M. (2004). Extreme Weather: A Guide & Record Book. United Kingdom: W.W. Norton.
Major Earthquake
Hanson, R. D. (1980). Northern Kentucky Earthquake, July 27, 1980. United States: Earthquake Engineering Research Institute
State Name Origin
Shearer, B. F., Shearer, B. S. (2001). State Names, Seals, Flags, and Symbols: A Historical Guide. United States: ABC-CLIO
State Nicknames
Shearer, B. F., Shearer, B. S. (2001). State Names, Seals, Flags, and Symbols: A Historical Guide. United States: ABC-CLIO
State Slogan
Shearer, B. F., Shearer, B. S. (2001). State Names, Seals, Flags, and Symbols: A Historical Guide. United States: ABC-CLIO
State Motto
TITLE I - SOVEREIGNTY AND JURISDICTION OF THE COMMONWEALTH. CHAPTER 2 -

CITIZENSHIP, EMBLEMS, HOLIDAYS, AND TIME. 2.020 State seal;
State Bird Research
TITLE I - SOVEREIGNTY AND JURISDICTION OF THE COMMONWEALTH. CHAPTER 2 - CITIZENSHIP, EMBLEMS, HOLIDAYS, AND TIME. SECTION 2.080. 2.080 State bird;
State Flag Illustration
"ST Abode Stock.com" Stock photos, royalty-free images,graphics,vectors,&videos; https://bit.ly/3iOnH08
State Flag Research
TITLE I - SOVEREIGNTY AND JURISDICTION OF THE COMMONWEALTH. CHAPTER 2 - CITIZENSHIP, EMBLEMS, HOLIDAYS, AND TIME. 2.030 State flag.;
State Flower Research
TITLE I - SOVEREIGNTY AND JURISDICTION OF THE COMMONWEALTH. CHAPTER 2 CITIZENSHIP, EMBLEMS, HOLIDAYS, AND TIME. SECTION 2.090. 2.090 State flower;
State Quarter Illustration
"ST Abode Stock.com" Stock photos, royalty-free images,graphics,vectors,&videos; https://bit.ly/3HgUi98
State Quarter Research
Noles, J. (2009). A Pocketful of History: Four Hundred Years of America--One State Quarter at a Time. United States: Hachette Books;
State Song Research
TITLE I - SOVEREIGNTY AND JURISDICTION OF THE COMMONWEALTH CHAPTER 002. CITIZENSHIP, EMBLEMS, HOLIDAYS, AND TIME SECTION 2.100. STATE SONG - BLUEGRASS SONG 2.100 State song - Bluegrass song;
State Tree Research
Kentucky Senate Bill No. 150 Chapter 43 (S.B. 150);
Twenty Interesting Facts Research
Brodowsky, P. K., Philbin, T., Churchill Downs, I. (2009). Two Minutes to Glory: The Official History of the Kentucky Derby. United States: HarperCollins.
Brown, A. (2021). Kentucky Legends and Lore. United States: History Press.
Applegate, K., Miller, J. (2009). Around Lake Cumberland. United States: Arcadia Pub..
Klass, R. (2005). Mammoth Cave National Park: Reflections. Ukraine: University Press of Kentucky.
Highway Accident Report. (1989). United States: National Transportation Safety Board..
The Kentucky Encyclopedia. (2014). United States: University Press of Kentucky.
Manning, R. (1999). The Historic Cumberland Plateau: An Explorer's Guide. United States: University of Tennessee Press.
DeSpain, J. Y., BurchJr., J. R., Hooper, T. Q. (2010). Campbellsville. United States: Arcadia Publishing Incorporated.
Douglas, E. M. (1939). Boundaries, Areas, Geographic Centers and Altitudes of the United States and Their Several States: With a Brief Record of Important Changes in Their Territory and Government. United States: U.S. Government Printing Office.
St. Mary's Cathedral Basilica of the Assumption (Covington, Ky.). (n.d.). United States: (n.p.).
Coleman Jr., J. W. (2012). Famous Kentucky Duels: The Story of the Code of Honor in the Bluegrass State. United States: Literary Licensing, LLC.
Bielo, J. S. (2018). Ark Encounter: The Making of a Creationist Theme Park. United States: NYU Press.
Congressional Record: Proceedings and Debates of the ... Congress. (2009). United States: U.S. Government Printing Office.
Cultivator and Country Gentleman. (1863). United States: Curtis Publishing Company.
Dudding, G. (2015). The Kelly-Hopkinsville UFO and Alien Shootout. United States: CreateSpace Independent Publishing Platform.
Crawford, B. (2001). Kentucky Stories. United States: Turner Publishing Company.
Kentucky's Last Great Places. (n.d.). (n.p.): University Press of Kentucky.
Ours, D. (2007). Man o' War: A Legend Like Lightning. United States: St. Martin's Publishing

RONDA SEXTON

Group.
Hearings, April 16 and 17, 1930. (1930). United States: U.S. Government Printing Office.
Rector, M. D. (2005). The United States Army at Fort Knox. United States: Arcadia.
Oldfield, M. (1999). The Millennium Bell. (n.p.): Warner.
Harrison, L. H., Klotter, J. C. (1997). A new history of Kentucky. United States: University Press of Kentucky.
Ten Crazy Laws
ARTICLE X. - CODE OF ETHICS[ DIVISION 1. - GENERALLY Sec. 2-776. - Conduct unbecoming (Ord. No. 2023-12-8799, § 1, 12-12-2023)
State of Kentucky, Title 304 | Chapter 001 | Regulation 020, Section 1
ARTICLE I. - IN GENERAL, ARTICLE II. - CURFEW FOR MINORS Sec. 9-23. - Same—Parent or guardian (Ord. No. 7-1997, § 3, 6-3-97)
City of Owensboro, Code of Ordinances; ARTICLE VIII. - TRADE PRACTICES Sec. 16-186. - Misuse of word "free, (Code 1955, § 21A-6)
Baldwin's Kentucky Revised Statutes Annotated. Title XL. Crimes and Punishments. Chapter 437. Offenses Against Public Peace; Conspiracies. 437.060 Use of reptiles in religious services
City of Georgetown, Code of Ordinances; Chapter 6 - ANIMALS ARTICLE II. - ANIMAL CONTROL Sec. 6-20. - General requirements (Code 1983, § 3-22; Ord. No. 04-027, § 2, 11-18-2004; Ord. No. 13-013, § 2, 6-24-2013)
State of Kentucky, Title 301 | Chapter 002 | Regulation 082, Section 4. Prohibited Species (2)
County of Hopkins, Code of Ordinances; Chapter 26 - SOLID WASTE, ARTICLE II. - STORAGE, COLLECTION AND DISPOSAL OF SOLID WASTE, Sec. 26-136. - Restrictions by composition of solid waste
State of Kentucky; Kentucky Marriage Laws § 402.105 Repealed and reenacted as this section 1984 Ky. Acts ch. 111, sec. 159, effective July 13, 1984. -- Recodified 1942 Ky. Acts ch. 208, sec. 1, effective October 1, 1942, from Ky. Stat. sec. 2105a-3.
State of Kentucky, Ky. Rev. Stat. § 436.140, "Repealed 1974 Ky. Acts ch. 406, sec. 336, effective 1/1/1975. --Recodified 1942 Ky. Acts ch. 208, sec. 1, effective 10/1/1942, from Ky. Stat. secs. 1376m-1, 1376m-2." Ky. Rev. Stat. § 436.140

Louisiana

Date of Statehood
Stienecker, D. L. (1996). First Facts about The States. United States: Scholastic
Rank of Admission
Stienecker, D. L. (1996). First Facts about The States. United States: Scholastic
State Capital
Aylesworth, T. G. (1990). State Capitals. United States: Gallery Books
State Capitol Building Architects
Cramer, J. P. (2005). Almanac of Architecture & Design, 2005. United States: Greenway Group
Population 2020
U.S Department of Commerce, United States Census Bureau (2020) Population and Housing State Data
Land Mass
U.S Department of Commerce, United States Census Bureau (2020) Population and Housing State Data
Highest Record Temperature
Burt, C. C., Stroud, M. (2004). Extreme Weather: A Guide & Record Book. United Kingdom: W.W. Norton.
Lowest Record Temperature
Burt, C. C., Stroud, M. (2004). Extreme Weather: A Guide & Record Book. United Kingdom: W.W. Norton.
Record Snowfall

National Oceanic and Atmospheric Adminstration, National Centers for Environmental Information {2020}: Snowfall Extremes
Record Precipitation
Burt, C. C., Stroud, M. (2004). Extreme Weather: A Guide & Record Book. United Kingdom: W.W. Norton.
Major Earthquake
Louisiana Earthquake, October 19, 1930, USCGS Cards. (1930). (n.p.): (n.p.)
State Name Origin
Shearer, B. F., Shearer, B. S. (2001). State Names, Seals, Flags, and Symbols: A Historical Guide. United States: ABC-CLIO
State Nicknames
Shearer, B. F., Shearer, B. S. (2001). State Names, Seals, Flags, and Symbols: A Historical Guide. United States: ABC-CLIO
State Slogan
Shearer, B. F., Shearer, B. S. (2001). State Names, Seals, Flags, and Symbols: A Historical Guide. United States: ABC-CLIO
State Motto
Louisiana Contitustion; TITLE 49 - State administration, RS 49:151 - State seal, Universal Citation: LA Rev Stat § 49:151 PART VIII. STATE SYMBOLS AND DISPLAY OF FLAGS §151. State seal
State Bird Research
Title 49 - State administration SECTION RS 49:159. §159. State bird
State Flag Illustration
"ST Abode Stock.com" Stock photos, royalty-free images,graphics,vectors,&videos;
State Flag Research
TITLE 49. State administration. RS 49:153 1 §153. State flag;
State Flower Research
TITLE 49 - State administration RS 49:154 - State flower Universal Citation: LA Rev Stat § 49:154 §154. State flower
State Quarter Illustration
"ST Abode Stock.com" Stock photos, royalty-free images,graphics,vectors,&videos
https://adobe.ly/3FvgyLf
State Quarter Research
Noles, J. (2009). A Pocketful of History: Four Hundred Years of America--One State Quarter at a Time. United States: Hachette Books;
State Song Research
Louisiana State Constitution; TITLE 49 - State administration, RS 49:155 - State song, Universal Citation: LA Rev Stat § 49:155 §155. State song Act 540, July 14, 1977
State Tree Research
TITLE 49 - State administration, RS 49:160 - State tree, Universal Citation: LA Rev Stat § 49:160 §160. State tree
Twenty Interesting Facts Research
The Louisiana Capitol: Its Art and Architecture. (1977). United States: Pelican Publishing.
Fortier, A. (1914). Louisiana: Comprising Sketches of Parishes, Towns, Events, Institutions, and Persons, Arranged in Cyclopedic Form. United States: Century historical association.
Hurricane Katrina: America's Unnatural Disaster. (2009). Ukraine: University of Nebraska Press.
Campanella, C. (2007). Lake Pontchartrain. United States: Arcadia Pub..
Flags of Louisiana. (1995). United States: Pelican Publishing.
In Search of Fundamental Law: Louisiana's Constitutions, 1812-1974. (1993). United States: Center for Louisiana Studies, University of Southwestern Louisiana.
Louisiana Almanac: 2006-2007. (2006). United States: Pelican Publishing Company.
Hartemann, F., Hauptman, R. (2005). The Mountain Encyclopedia: An A to Z Compendium of Over 2,250 Terms, Concepts, Ideas, and People. United States: Taylor Trade Publishing.
Butts, M. (2011). Grunch Road: A Novel. (n.p.): CreateSpace Independent Publishing Platform.

Brasseaux, C. A. (2005). French, Cajun, Creole, Houma: A Primer on Francophone Louisiana. United Kingdom: LSU Press.
Alderson, D. (2020). America's Alligator: A Popular History of Our Most Celebrated Reptile. United States: Globe Pequot.
Symeonides, S. C. (1988). An Introduction to the Louisiana Civil Law System. United States: LSU Paul M. Herbert Law Center Publications Institute.
Burgan, M. (2002). The Louisiana Purchase. United States: Compass Point Books.
Whole Country in Commotion: the Lousiana Purchase & the American Southwest (p). (2005). United States: University of Arkansas Press.
Stuart, B. (2012). Louisiana Curiosities: Quirky Characters, Roadside Oddities & Other Offbeat Stuff. United States: Globe Pequot.
Burns, A. C. (1994). A History of the Kisatchie National Forest. United States: U.S. Department of Agriculture, Forest Service, Southern Region, Kisatchie National Forest.
Nichols, M. W. (1981). The Jefferson Island Mine Inundation: Report of Mine Inundation, Jefferson Island Mine, Diamond Crystal Salt Company, New Iberia, Iberia Parish, Louisiana, November 20, 1980. United States: U.S. Department of Labor, Mine Safety and Health Administration.
Mississippi River Ports Below and Above New Orleans, Louisiana. (2003). United States: U.S. Army, Corps of Engineers.
Alford, K., ABBOTT, B. (2012). Bottom of Da Boot: Louisiana's Disappearing Coast. United States: Fall Line Arts Press.
Costello, B. J. (2017). Carnival in Louisiana: Celebrating Mardi Gras from the French Quarter to the Red River. United States: LSU Press.
Piazza, B. P. (2014). The Atchafalaya River Basin: History and Ecology of an American Wetland. United States: Texas A&M University Press.
Ten Crazy Laws
Louisiana; 2006 Louisiana Laws - RS 14:67.13 — Theft of an alligator, §67.13. Theft of an alligator
City of Zachary, Code of Ordinances; Chapter 58 - OFFENSES AND MISCELLANEOUS PROVISIONS, ARTICLE III. - CULPABILITY, Sec. 58-18. - Justification generally, Sec. 58-21. - Aggressor cannot claim self-defense
Amite City, Code of Ordinances; CHAPTER 5. - CRIMES AGAINST THE HEALTH, WELFARE AND MORALS, Section 11-5017. - Minors under sixteen to be permitted in pool or billiard rooms or bowling alleys., § 11-6001
Parish of New Orleans; Code of Ordinances; ARTICLE III. - EXHIBITIONS AND DISPLAYS, Sec. 18-136. - Wild, exotic, etc., animals—Keeping prohibited (Code 1956, § 7-17(c); M.C.S., Ord. No. 25205, § 1, 3-7-13)
Louisiana; 4. Preservation of Linguistic and Cultural Origins, Section 4.
Louisiana; Chapter 6 - ANIMALS ARTICLE I. - IN GENERAL Sec. 6-4. - Keeping of swine.,(Code 1979, § 4-5; Ord. No. 94-2, 5-4-1994)
City of New Orleans, Code of Ordinances; NO. R-00-169, Section 34-27 of Chapter 34 of the Code of the City of New Orleans entitled Prohibited Throws
City of Lafeyette, Code of Ordinances; DIVISION 2. - SPECIFIC CRIMES AND OFFENSES IN CITY OF LAFAYETTE, Sec. 62-64. - Same—Trespassing on, damaging, tampering with property and appurtenances. (City Code 1965, § 10-64)
Assumption Parish, Louisiana, Code of Ordinances; SUB-CHAPTER D. - EMPLOYEE HOUSING FACILITIES, Sec. 11-203. - Responsibility for operation and provision of interpreter requirement. (Ord. No. 07-02, 1-11-07)
Caddo Parish, Code of Ordinances; Chapter 32 - OFFENSES AND MISCELLANEOUS PROVISIONS, ARTICLE II. - OFFENSES AFFECTING PUBLIC MORALS, Sec. 32-22. - Wearing of pants below waist in public.(Ord. No. 5245, 11-8-2012)

Maine

Date of Statehood
Stienecker, D. L. (1996). First Facts about The States. United States: Scholastic
Rank of Admission
Stienecker, D. L. (1996). First Facts about The States. United States: Scholastic
State Capital
Aylesworth, T. G. (1990). State Capitals. United States: Gallery Book
State Capitol Building Architects
Elliott, C. D. (2003). The American Architect from the Colonial Era to the Present. United Kingdom: McFarland, Incorporated, Publishers
Population 2020
U.S Department of Commerce, United States Census Bureau (2020) Population and Housing State Data
Land Mass
U.S Department of Commerce, United States Census Bureau (2020) Population and Housing State Data
Highest Record Temperature
Burt, C. C., Stroud, M. (2004). Extreme Weather: A Guide & Record Book. United Kingdom: W.W. Norton.
Lowest Record Temperature
Calhoun, A., Redford, K. (2023). Our Maine: Exploring Its Rich Natural Heritage. United States: Down East Books.
Record Snowfall
Burt, C. C., Stroud, M. (2004). Extreme Weather: A Guide & Record Book. United Kingdom: W.W. Norton.
Record Precipitation
Burt, C. C., Stroud, M. (2004). Extreme Weather: A Guide & Record Book. United Kingdom: W.W. Norton
Major Earthquake
Earthquakes in Maine. (1989). United States: The Survey
State Name Origin
Shearer, B. F., Shearer, B. S. (2001). State Names, Seals, Flags, and Symbols: A Historical Guide. United States: ABC-CLIO
State Nicknames
Shearer, B. F., Shearer, B. S. (2001). State Names, Seals, Flags, and Symbols: A Historical Guide. United States: ABC-CLIO
State Slogan
Shearer, B. F., Shearer, B. S. (2001). State Names, Seals, Flags, and Symbols: A Historical Guide. United States: ABC-CLIO
State Motto
Title 1: GENERAL PROVISIONS, Chapter 9: SEAL, MOTTO, EMBLEMS AND FLAGS
Subchapter 1: GENERAL PROVISIONS, §205. State motto
State Bird Research
TITLE 1. GENERAL PROVISIONS. CHAPTER 9. SEAL, MOTTO, EMBLEMS AND FLAGS. SECTION 209. §209. State bird
State Flag Illustration
"ST Abode Stock.com" Stock photos, royalty-free images,graphics,vectors,&videos
State Flag Research
Title 1: GENERAL PROVISIONS, Chapter 9: SEAL, MOTTO, EMBLEMS AND FLAGS
Subchapter 1: GENERAL PROVISIONS, §206. State flag
State Flower Research
Title 1: GENERAL PROVISIONS.Chapter 9: SEAL, MOTTO, EMBLEMS AND FLAGS.
Subchapter 1: GENERAL PROVISIONS. SECTION 211. §211. State flower
State Quarter Illustration

"ST Abode Stock.com" Stock photos, royalty-free images,graphics,vectors,&videos; https://bit.ly/3iMefe1
State Quarter Research
Noles, J. (2009). A Pocketful of History: Four Hundred Years of America--One State Quarter at a Time. United States: Hachette Books;
State Song Research
Title 1: GENERAL PROVISIONS, Chapter 9: SEAL, MOTTO, EMBLEMS AND FLAGS
Subchapter 1: GENERAL PROVISIONS, Section 210
State Tree Research
Title 1: GENERAL PROVISIONS, Chapter 9: SEAL, MOTTO, EMBLEMS AND FLAGS
Subchapter 1: GENERAL PROVISIONS, §208. State tree
Twenty Interesting Facts Research
Vieira, M. J., Conway, J. N. (2017). New England Rocks: Historic Geological Wonders. United States: History Press.
Benton-Short, L., Short, J. R., Mayda, C. (2018). A Regional Geography of the United States and Canada: Toward a Sustainable Future. United States: Rowman & Littlefield Publishers.
Longshore, D. (2010). Encyclopedia of Hurricanes, Typhoons, and Cyclones, New Edition. United States: Facts On File, Incorporated.
U.S Department of Commerce, United States Census Bureau (2020) Population and Housing
Chase, R., Chase, N. (2012). Mountains for Mortals: New England: Scenic Summits for Hikers. United Kingdom: Menasha Ridge Press.
Pierson, E. (1996). A Birder's Guide to Maine. United States: Down East Books.
Schmitt, C. (2016). Historic Acadia National Park: The Stories Behind One of America's Great Treasures. United States: Lyons Press.
The World Almanac and Book of Facts. (1942). United States: Press Publishing Company (The New York World).
Sleeper, F. H. (2002). Baxter State Park and the Allagash River. United States: Arcadia Pub..
Burk, J. S. (2011). The Wildlife of New England: A Viewer's Guide. Lebanon: University of New Hampshire Press.
White Mountain National Forest (N.F.), Forest Plan Revision, Proposed Land and Resource Management Plan: Environmental Impact Statement. (2005). United States: (n.p.).\
Connors, K. (2015). Acadia National Park. United States: Gareth Stevens Publishing.
Parks and People: Managing Outdoor Recreation at Acadia National Park. (2009). Lebanon: University of Vermont Press.
Synoptic-Dynamic Meteorology and Weather Analysis and Forecasting: A Tribute to Fred Sanders. (1987). Netherlands: American Meteorological Society.
Peterson, S. (2008). Maine. United States: Creative Education.
Geographical Review. (1924). United States: American Geographical Society..
Saint Croix Island International Historic Site General Management Plan: Environmental Impact Statement. (1998). United States: (n.p.).
Water Resources Development: Maine. (1973). United States: U.S. Army Engineer Division, New England.
Maine: The Pine Tree State. (2008). United Kingdom: Encyclopaedia Britannica, Incorporated.
Heffernan, M. (2010). Fairy Houses of the Maine Coast. United States: Down East Books
Butler, J. (2014). Wildfire Loose: The Week Maine Burned. United States: Down East Books.
Brunet-Jailly, E. (2015). Border Disputes: A Global Encyclopedia [3 Volumes]. United States: ABC-CLIO.
Westrich, G. (2020). Hiking Waterfalls Maine: A Guide to the State's Best Waterfall Hikes. United States: Falcon Guides.
Knoblock, G. A. (2012). Historic Iron and Steel Bridges in Maine, New Hampshire and Vermont. United Kingdom: McFarland, Incorporated, Publishers.
Dornfeld, M., Hart, J. (2010). Maine. United States: Marshall Cavendish Benchmark.
Ten Crazy Laws
City of Auburn, Code of Ordinances; Chapter 34 - PARKS, RECREATION, FACILITIES AND SPECIAL

EVENTS[1], ARTICLE III. - RULES AND REGULATIONS, Sec. 34-50. - Protection of park property, (Ord. No. 13-04042022, 4-19-2022)
Town of Freeport, Code of Ordinances; CHAPTER 33  STYROFOAM ORDINANCE
Town of Old Orchard Beach, Code of Ordinances; Chapter 38 - OFFENSES AND MISCELLANEOUS PROVISIONS[1], ARTICLE VIII. - NEWSPAPER VENDING MACHINES, Sec. 38-281. - Purpose. (Ord. of 3-21-06(2))
Town of Eliot, Code of Ordinances; Chapter 7 - ANIMAL CONTROL, Sec. 7-8. - Animal noise, (T.M. of 7-14-2020(1))
State of Maine; Article II. Electors. Indians.
State of Maine; MAINE STATUES REGARDING CEMETERIES AND BURIAL GROUNDS, 13 § 1266. Solicitation of cemetery or crematory services or property
State of Maine; Section 25. Right to food.
Town of Waterboro, Code of Ordinances; Title: Regulation of Parks and Recreational Spaces, Section 1 – GENERAL REGULATIONS, 1.01.10
Town of Orono, Code of Ordinances; Chapter 3 - ADDRESSING, [Sec. 3-4. - Naming system, (Ord. of 7-10-96)
Town of Brunswick, Code of Ordinances; Chapter 6 - CABLE TELEVISION[1], Sec. 6-9. - Hours of operation, (Ord. of 4-22-03)

## Maryland

Date of Statehood
Stienecker, D. L. (1996). First Facts about The States. United States: Scholastic
Rank of Admission
Stienecker, D. L. (1996). First Facts about The States. United States: Scholastic
State Capital
Aylesworth, T. G. (1990). State Capitals. United States: Gallery Books
State Capitol Building Architects
Goodsell, C. T. (2001). The American statehouse : interpreting democracy's temples. United Kingdom: University Press of Kansas
Population 2020
U.S Department of Commerce, United States Census Bureau (2020) Population and Housing State Data
Land Mass
U.S Department of Commerce, United States Census Bureau (2020) Population and Housing State Data
Highest Record Temperature
Burt, C. C., Stroud, M. (2004). Extreme Weather: A Guide & Record Book. United Kingdom: W.W. Norton.
Lowest Record Temperature
Burt, C. C., Stroud, M. (2004). Extreme Weather: A Guide & Record Book. United Kingdom: W.W. Norton.
Record Snowfall
Burt, C. C., Stroud, M. (2004). Extreme Weather: A Guide & Record Book. United Kingdom: W.W. Norton.
Record Precipitation
Burt, C. C., Stroud, M. (2004). Extreme Weather: A Guide & Record Book. United Kingdom: W.W. Norton.
Major Earthquake
Earthquake Research and Analysis: New Frontiers in Seismology. (2012). Croatia: IntechOpen
State Name Origin
Shearer, B. F., Shearer, B. S. (2001). State Names, Seals, Flags, and Symbols: A Historical Guide. United States: ABC-CLIO

State Nicknames
Shearer, B. F., Shearer, B. S. (2001). State Names, Seals, Flags, and Symbols: A Historical Guide. United States: ABC-CLIO
State Slogan
Shearer, B. F., Shearer, B. S. (2001). State Names, Seals, Flags, and Symbols: A Historical Guide. United States: ABC-CLIO
State Motto
TITLE 13. EMBLEMS; COMMEMORATIVE DAYS; MANUAL. Subtitle 1. State Seal.
SECTION 13.102. § 13-102. Description of Great Seal
State Bird Research
(Chapter 54, Acts of 1947; Code General Provisions Article, sec. 7-301).
State Flag Illustration
"ST Abode Stock.com" Stock photos, royalty-free images,graphics,vectors,&videos
State Flag Research
(Chapter 48, Acts of 1904, effective March 9, 1904
State Flower Research
General Assembly (Chapter 458, Acts of 1918; Code General Provisions Article, sec. 7-306).
State Quarter Illustration
"ST Abode Stock.com" Stock photos, royalty-free images,graphics,vectors,&videos; https://bit.ly/3Uzv2xT
State Quarter Research
Noles, J. (2009). A Pocketful of History: Four Hundred Years of America--One State Quarter at a Time. United States: Hachette Books
State Song Research
General Assembly (Chapter 451, Acts of 1939; Code General Provisions Article, sec. 7-318).
State Tree Research
(Chapter 731, Acts of 1941; Code General Provisions Article, sec. 7-310).
Twenty Interesting Facts Research
Franz, R., Slifer, D. (1971). Caves of Maryland. United States: Maryland Geological Survey.
State Park Statistics. (1958). United States: U.S. Department of the Interior, National Park Service, Recreational Planning Division.
The National Road: Maryland, Pennsylvania, West Virginia, Ohio, Indiana, Illinois. (1994). United States: U.S. Department of the Interior, Southwestern Pennsylvania Heritage Preservation Commission, National Park Service.
Otfinoski, S., Steinitz, A. (2011). Maryland. United States: Marshall Cavendish Benchmark.
Deep Creek Lake: Environmental Impact Statement. (1972). United States: (n.p.).
Ernst, H. R. (2003). Chesapeake Bay Blues: Science, Politics, and the Struggle to Save the Bay. United Kingdom: Rowman & Littlefield Publishers.
Antietam, National Battlefield Site, Maryland. (1941). United States: U.S. Government Printing Office.
Chapelle, S. E. (2010). Maryland Government. United States: Gibbs Smith Publishers.
Maryland Toleration Act. (2009). (n.p.): Great Neck Pub..
Field Excursions to the Appalachian Plateaus and the Valley and Ridge for GSA Connects 2023. (2023). United States: Geological Society of America.
Doheny, E. J., Nealen, C. W. (2021). Storms and Floods of July 30, 2016, and May 27, 2018, in Ellicott City, Maryland. United States: U.S. Department of the Interior, U.S. Geological Survey.
Elliot, J. (1830). Historical Sketches of the Ten Miles Square Forming the District of Columbia. United States: J. Elliot, Jr..
Arnett, E., Brugger, R. J., Papenfuse, E. C. (1999). Maryland: A New Guide to the Old Line State. United Kingdom: Johns Hopkins University Press.
Blank, T. J., Puglia, D. J. (2014). Maryland Legends: Folklore from the Old Line State. United States: Arcadia Publishing Incorporated.
Brown, S. E. (2014). Hiking Maryland: A Guide for Hikers and Photographers. United States: Stackpole Books.

Schwartz, R., Karr, A., Myatt, K. (2007). Hurricanes and the Middle Atlantic States. United States: Blue Diamond Books.
Hurricane Irene, August 21-30, 2011. (2012). United States: U.S. Department of Commerce, National Oceanic and Atmospheric Administration, National Weather Service.
DiLisio, J. (2014). Maryland Geography: An Introduction. United States: Johns Hopkins University Press.
Leigh, E. G. (1999). Tropical Forest Ecology: A View from Barro Colorado Island. United Kingdom: Oxford University Press.
Balkan, E. (2011). The Best in Tent Camping: Maryland: A Guide for Car Campers Who Hate RVs, Concrete Slabs, and Loud Portable Stereos. United Kingdom: Menasha Ridge Press.
The Baltimore Conflagration: Report of the Committee on Fire-Restrictive Construction of the National Fire Protection Association, 1904. (1904). United States: Office of the Secretary of the Association.
Hamilton, J. (2016). Maryland. United States: ABDO Publishing Company.
Horton, T. (1996). An Island Out of Time: A Memoir of Smith Island in the Chesapeake. United Kingdom: W.W. Norton.
Amos, W. H. (1980). Assateague Island National Seashore, Maryland and Virginia. United States: The Division.
Here In America. (n.d.). (n.p.): Xlibris Corporation.
Ten Crazy Laws
Town of Chevy Chase, Code of Ordinances; Chapter 15 - MOTOR VEHICLES AND TRAFFIC[, ARTICLE II. - STOPPING, STANDING AND PARKING[2], DIVISION 2. - PERMIT PARKING, (Code 1964, § 9A(b)—(f); Ord. No. 19-04, § 1, 4-24-19)
City of Mount Rainer, Code of Ordinances; CHAPTER 12B - URBAN FOREST, Section 12B-7. - Private property—Tree work for hire in the City.
Town of Woodsboro, Code of Ordinances; Chapter 14 - NUISANCES, ARTICLE II. - HEALTH NUISANCES, Sec. 14-22. - Removal of rubbish and waste. (Code 1992, § 115-1)
City of Gaithersburg, Code of Ordinances; ARTICLE I. - SOLID WASTE COLLECTION AND DISPOSAL, Sec. 18-6. - Recyclable solid waste—Definition, (Ord. No. O-8-93, 5-3-93)
Baltimore County, Code of Ordinances; TITLE 5. - LIVABILITY CODE, SUBTITLE 1. - IN GENERAL, § 35-5-212. - MECHANICAL AND ELECTRICAL REQUIREMENTS.(1988 Code, § 18-81) (Bill No. 69-95, § 7, 7-1-1995; Bill No. 46-96, § 3, 1-1-1997; Bill No. 25-01, § 2, 7-1-2004)
Town of La Plata, Code of Ordinances; Chapter 8 - BEAUTIFICATION COMMISSION, 8-6 - Compensation
St. Mary's County, Code of Ordinances; Chapter 260 - REMOVAL OF FROZEN PRECIPITATION FROM PUBLIC SIDEWALKS AND STREETS[1], Sec. 260-2. - Removal of snow, ice or other frozen precipitation. (Amended 3-22-2016 by § III of Ord. No. 2016-07)
City of Frostburg, Code of Ordinances; Article 2 - POLICE AND PUBLIC PEACE, Sec. 2-5. - Unruly social gatherings, ( Ord. No. 2019-01, § 2, 3-21-2019 )
Town of Ocean City, Code of Ordinances; Chapter 6 - ANIMALS, ARTICLE I. - IN GENERAL, Sec. 6-1. - Keeping reptiles or other nondomesticated animals.(Code 1972, § 23-6; Code 1999, § 6-1; Ord. No. 2010-17, 6-7-2010; Ord. No. 2012-1, 2-6-2012; Ord. No. 2022-12 , 5-16-2022)
Prince George County, Code of Ordinances; DIVISION 5. - PEST CONTROL., SUBDIVISION 1. - GENERAL PROVISIONS, Sec. 12-137. - Rodent-proof construction of structures. (Ord. and Res. 1963, Sec. 9-11; CB-127-1987)

www.ingramcontent.com/pod-product-compliance
Lightning Source LLC
Chambersburg PA
CBHW060832190426
43197CB00039B/2566